Hide 'n' Seek Kids

Volume I
Visual Aids, ESV
Units I-4

Constance Dever ©2016 Praise Factory Media

manufacturers of active minds, noisy joy, and prayerful hearts since 1997

Curriculum for preschool and elementary age children,
training tools, music and other resources
are available for download or to order at:
www.praisefactory.org

Table of Contents

Unit 4 Visual Aids

Getting Started with Hide 'n' Seek Kids

Get It

Order the **<u>Praise Factory Tour: Extended Version</u>** (or download it from the website in the Getting Started with Hide 'n' Seek Kids section). It is going to be your easiest, most visual way to learn about this curriculum. Order/download the **<u>Hide 'n' Seek Kids Core Curriculum (ESV/NIV)</u>** and the **<u>Hide 'n' Seek Kids Visual Aids books (Small Format/Large Format pictures)</u>** resources.

Tour It....Three Times

1 **1. Read through the whole Praise Factory Tour: Extended Version book once.**
Learn how each curriculum in the Praise Factory family is related to each other. Pay special attention to the section on Hide 'n' Seek Kids.

2 **2. Go back and read through just the section on Hide 'n' Seek Kids in the Tour book again.**

3 **3. Now go back and read the Hide 'n' Seek section of the Tour book a third time, only this time, get out your two resource books (Hide 'n' Seek Kids Core Curriculum and Hide 'n' Seek Kids Visual Aids books) and follow along.**
This will help you see how the curriculum flows and where to find each of the resources visualized in the Tour Book.

Rip It Up

The **<u>Hide 'n' Seek Kids Visual Aids book</u>** is meant to be taken apart. These will be made into your visual aids and storyboard pictures used in each lesson.

You May Want to Second It

The **Hide 'n' Seek Kids Core Curriculum book** contains resources you will probably want to photocopy--such as, the lesson plans, the crafts/take home sheets, and the music for the songs. **For this reason, you might want to print out a second copy (from online) or buy a second copy of the book.** This will allow you to take apart one copy for easy photocopying and still have another one intact for reference. Or, you can photocopy a copy from your original and keep that on hand.

Choose It

Choose how you want to use the curriculum resources with your kids and your setting. There is a questionaire and other resources in the Getting Started section of the praisefactory.org website that can help you make the best custom fit for your situation. You may want to follow the curriculum as written and use them all. Or, you may want to pick and choose. Do what is best for your situation.

Prepare It and Protect It

Cut out and laminate the Big Question Box resources (Big Question and Answer; Bible Verse; and, Listening Assignment signs) as well as the storyboard pictures from the **Hide 'n' Seek Kids Visual Aids book.** Stick velcro on the back of the storyboard pictures to get them ready to be used on the storyboard and in the Story Review games. **More information about making storyboard pictures can be found in Appendix E of the Core Curriculum books.**

Download It

Download the **zip file of unit songs** from the website.

Getting Started with Hide 'n' Seek Kids, continued

Make It... Before You Get Started

There are a few more resources that Hide 'n' Seek Kids uses that you will need to make before you use the curriculum. You need to purchase/make a **Big Question Box; a HSK "Bible" folder; and a flannelgraph storyboard**. Directions for making these are found in the **back of the Core Curriculum books in Appendix E.**

Are You Game?

There is one more set of resources you will be glad you made ahead of time: the games! Hide 'n' Seek Kids is a very active curriculum, with a number of different games suggested for each lesson. The good news is that they are used in a rotation throughout the curriculum. That means, once you make these games, you store them and use them over and over (and for years to come!).

While you only need to make whatever games you choose to use with each lesson, **I strongly recommend that you make all the games before you start using the curriculum.** Get the prep work over with at the beginning and coast your way through years of enjoyment!

Store them in ziploc bags or baskets and pull them out when needed. So simple! Your teachers will love how easy it is to have an engaging learning session with so little work for them to do! Happy teachers are more likeyly to be repeat teachers! **A full list of the games and the supplies needed to make them can be found in the back of the Core Curriculum books in Appendix B with the instructions for all the games.**

Session Prep

Prepare the curriculum for your teachers. Largely, this will mean making copies of the lesson plan, the crafts and take home sheets...especially if you have already assembled the games. We give the teachers a **basket of curriculum and materials they will use to teach the class each session.** This has worked very well for us.

Don't Ignore It, Store It!

This is a curriculum that keeps on giving, year after year. If you do a good job of storing the curriculum, it will serve your church well and at little cost for many years. We store the resources for each unit in **manilla envelopes and magazine storage boxes.**

Learn More

There are many more resources online that may help you customize the curriculum to fit your learning situation. These are listed online in the Praise Factory Resources section, as well as in the Getting Started section.
Two you might especially want to look at are:
- **From the Ground Up** (Making a Great Start in Children's Ministry and with the Praise Factory Family of Curriculum)
- **Classroom Management Suggestions for Teaching Preschoolers**
These are available for download or to order through Amazon.com.

See It in Action

visit us in
Washington,
D.C.

Three times a year (the third Saturday/Sunday of March, May and September), we hold a **free lunch, learn-and-look workshop and observation time here at Capitol Hill Baptist Church in Washington, D.C.**

On the Saturday, we gather for lunch and talk philosophy, child protection policy, encouraging parents, dealing with discipline issues, etc. and, of course, curriculum. After finishing up our group session, we are happy to talk to individual churches about their particular situations. Then on Sunday, we offer an opportunity to see Hide 'n' Seek Kids and the other Praise Factory curriculum in action in our classes. The registration form for these workshops can be found on the Praise Factory website.

Hide 'n' Seek Kids

Unit I
Visual Aids

About the Hide 'n' Seek Kids Visual Aids

How Are They Used?

 The Hide 'n' Seek Visual Aids book is a companion resource to be used alongside the Hide 'n' Seek Kids Core Curriculum book for each unit. These colorful pictures are used in presenting the key concepts; telling the Bible stories; and, in playing the Bible Story Review games.

What Do They Include?

There are five, different resources included in this book:

1. Key Concept Visual Aids-- colorful signs of the Big Question and Answer, the Bible verse, and the Listening Assignments to use with the 5 lessons for each unit.

2. The Storyboard Picture Key-a who's who of the pictures in thumbnail size. Some pictures are labelled "BG." These are your background pictures that you put on the storyboard before telling the story. The rest of the pictures are labelled "SB." These are pictures you put up on the storyboard as you tell the story.

3. Storyboard Suggested Picture Placement page--where to place the pictures on your storyboard.

4. The pictures, themselves. Notice that each picture is identified and numbered on the back for easy reference. The numbers corrrespond to the numbers in the Picture Placement Key and in the actually story script (found in the Core Curriculum book.)

5. Directions for making the Hide 'n' Seek Kids "Bible" Folder and the **back/front images** to paste in place when making it. (Larger back/front images are found online with the curriculum.)

(Directions for how to make a homemade flannelgraph storyboard and sturdy storyboard pictures are found in **Appendix E in the Core Curriculum book.)**

Ready, Set, Rip It Out!

 This book is meant to be ripped up and made into your visual aids. The key concept signs can be cut out and laminated or slipped into sheet protectors. Cut out around the storyboard images and ideally, laminate these. Some of the biggest pictures actually need to be stuck together, before laminating.

Store It!

 Hide 'n' Seek Kids is a curriculum that can be used over and over. Store your visual aids and storyboard pictures after using them and they will serve you for many years. We store ours in manilla envelopes and then put them (along with all the rest of the curriculum) in magazine files, labelled by unit. If you have multiple classes using the curriculum, store each set of resources in separate manilla envelopes. This will make prep much simpler, second time around.

Replacement Storyboard Pictures

You can always purchase this book again or simply go online and print out any pictures that go missing.

Two Sizes of Storyboard Pictures

There are two sizes of storyboard pictures to choose from: the standard, large format pictures; or, the smaller format pictures. The larger pictures are best for a big classroom and a storyboard that is at least 36" x 48." (We actually make a whole section of a wall into a felt storyboard!) The small format pictures are created to fit smaller storyboards--in the 24" x 36" to 36" by 48" range. They are most useful in the smaller class or for use at home.

The Case of the Old Man Who Looked for God
Luke 2:25-32

Story-telling Tips

Ahead of time:
1. Read the Bible verses and story. Pray!
2. Choose story action cues and/or prepare storyboard pictures, if using. (Included in Visual Aids book)
3. Practice telling story with the pictures, timing your presentation. Shorten, if necessary to fit your allotted time.

During your presentation:
1. Maintain as much eye contact as possible as you tell the story.
2. Put up storyboard figures/add story action cues as you tell the story. Allow the children to help you put them on the board, if desired.
3. Include the children in your story with a few questions about what they think will happen or words/concepts that might be new to them.
4. Watch the kids for signs that their attention span has been reached. Shorten, if necessary.

INTRODUCTION/ LISTENING ASSIGNMENTS

"Our story is called: The Case of the Old Man Who Looked for God. Here is your listening assignment... "

Read from Detective Dan's Listening Assignment signs, but questions are summarized below:

Detective Dan's Lesson #1 Listening Assignment:

I need to find out:
1. Who was the old man who looked for God?
2. How did he find out what God was like?

Detective Dan's Lesson #2 Listening Assignment:

Our Bible verse is Amos 4:13: "He who declares to man what is His thought...The LORD, the God of hosts, is His name."

I need to find out:
1. Who did the LORD declare His thoughts to?
2. What book did the LORD use to declare His thoughts?

Detective Dan's Lesson #3 Listening Assignment:

I found four clues, but one of them is NOT in the story.
They are: baby Jesus, a chair, God's Word (on a scroll, like in Bible times) and a heart.
Hold up each of the four pictures for the children to see as you identify them. Better yet, put them up on your flannelgraph storyboard, off to one side.

I need to figure out:
1. Which three pictures belong in the story and which one does not?
2. What did God use three of these things to show Simeon?

Detective Dan's Lesson #4 Listening Assignment:

I need to find out:
1. Who did Simeon want to know more and more?
2. What was something Simeon thanked God for?

Detective Dan's Lesson #5 Listening Assignment:

I need to find out:
1. Why was Simeon so happy to see baby Jesus?
2. What did God send Jesus to do?

Read the questions, THEN SAY,

"Ok, Hide 'n' Seekers! Put on your best listening ears and see if you can find the answers to Detective Dan's questions. When I finish telling the story, we'll see what we come up with."

"The Case of the Old Man Who Looked for God" Luke 2:25-32

Story with lines separating paragraphs (text in bold, optional interaction cues in italics) Numbers correspond to storyboard pictures and placement upon the storyboard. Alway feel free to use less pictures, if it's best for your kids. Simply, black out the numbers next to pictures you do not plan to use. All pictures are found in the Visual Aids book. Put BG (background) pictures on storyboard ahead of time. SB pictures (listed below in story text) are added to board as you tell the story. These numbers are also found on the back of each picture.
Tip: Stack pictures in numerical order before telling story for easy use. Use sticky-back velcro to attach pictures to storyboard felt. Use sticky-tac putty to stick a picture on top of another picture.

Simeon (SB1) was a very, very old man.

Have you seen a very old man? They often have gray hair and sometimes even have a long, grey beard. Simeon looked like that!

Simeon knew and loved God in his heart (SB2).

Can you point to where your heart is?

But oh, how Simeon wanted to know more about what God is like!

Simeon looked around him at God's beautiful world. There was so much to see! There was so much to see!

The big, tall mountains,

Can you stretch up your arms really high like a tall mountain?

the (SB3) galloping horses,

When horses gallop they run really, really fast and make lots of noise with their feet. Can you stomp your feet like you were a galloping horse?

the (SB4) flying birds,

Let's flap our arms like birds!

the (SB5) buzzing bees.

What sound does a buzzing bee make?

Simeon could see how wonderful God was in all the things He had made. But oh, how Simeon wanted to know more about what God is like!

Simeon listened to the Bible (SB6), too.

Where's our Bible? Have children point to your Bible.

He heard that God was loving and good and very, very strong.

But oh, how Simeon wanted to know more about what God is like!

*Story with lines separating paragraphs (**text in bold,** optional interaction cues in italics)*

Then one day something very, very good happened to Simeon. God gave Simeon a wonderful promise: "I am sending My Son, Jesus here to earth. He will show people what I am like and bring them to know and love Me. He will bring My forgiveness to everyone who trusts in Him as their Savior! They will know Me in their heart. Then one day, they will come to live happily with Me forever!" God promised. "And Simeon, you will get to see My Son, Jesus at my Temple-Church before you die!" God told Simeon.

Simeon gathered with other people to worship God at a special place called the Temple. Where do we gather together to worship God? Why, it's right here! We're in it now! It's a church!

How excited Simeon was! Oh, how wonderful it would be to see God's very own Son!

Simeon went to God's Temple-Church.

Walk! Walk! Walk! Here goes Simeon to God's Temple-Church. Can you make a walking noise with your feet?

And who did Simeon see when he got there? Mary and Joseph (SB7). And who were they carrying? Baby Jesus, God's Son!

Pretend to hold a baby in your arms.

Simeon was very happy to see baby Jesus, God's Son, just as God had promised!

Yes, there was Jesus, just a little baby! But Jesus wouldn't stay a baby. He would grow up, up, up (SB8). He would tell everyone about God (SB9). He would show them what God is like. And, He would die on the cross to save God's people. They would be forgiven by God for disobeying Him! Yay!

Let's cheer really loud! Yay!

Then on Day One, Two, Three, (SB10) Jesus would rise up from the dead, showing He had really done it! Yes, God's people were forgiven! Jesus had beaten sin and death for them! Yay!

Let's cheer really loud again! Yay!

One day, old Simeon died (SB11). Was that a sad day for Simeon? No, it was not!

Shake your head "no."

That was the day when God brought (SB12) Simeon to live with Him always. There, Simeon would live with (SB13) Jesus forever. This was the happiest day of all.

Now Simeon would really get to know how wonderful God is...forever and ever!

Simeon is so happy in heaven where he lives happily with God forever. Let's cheer really loud! Yay!

Cracking the Case: (story wrap-up for Listening Assignments)

It's time to see how we did with our Listening Assignment.

Detective Dan's Lesson #1 Listening Assignment:
1. Who was the old man who looked for God?
Simeon.
2. How did he find out what God was like?
He knew God in his heart; he saw what God was like as he looked around him at the things God had made; he learned about Him in the Bible, God's Word; and most of all, he knew what God was like through His Son, Jesus.

For You and Me:
Like Simeon, we can know what God is like. God has given us a heart to know and love Him. We can look around us and see what He's like in the things He has made. We can learn about Him in the Bible; and, we can know what He's like most of all when we learn about Jesus. We can ask God to show us what He's like and help us to know and love Him. He delights to do this!

Detective Dan's Lesson #2 Listening Assignment:

Our Bible Verse is: Amos 4:13:
"He who declares to man what is His thought...The LORD, the God of hosts, is His name."

1. Who did the LORD declare His thoughts to?
Simeon.
2. What book did the LORD use to declare His thoughts? The Bible, God's Word.

For You and Me:
The LORD can show us what He's like as we look around at all the amazing things He has made. He can declare His thoughts to us as we read the Bible, His Word and learn about His Son, Jesus Ask God to show Himself to you! He delights to do this!

Detective Dan's Lesson #3 Listening Assignment:
I found four clues, but one of them is NOT in the story. They are: baby Jesus, a chair, God's Word (on a scroll, like in Bible times) and a heart.

I need to know:
1. Which three pictures belong in the story and which one does not? The chair does not belong.
2. What did God use three of these things to show Simeon? God used baby Jesus, the Bible and the heart He gave Simeon to show Simeon what He is like.

For You and Me:
The LORD wants to show us what He's like, too. He can use the heart He's given us, the Bible, and Jesus to show us what He's like, too.

Detective Dan's Lesson #4 Listening Assignment:
1. Who did Simeon want to know more and more about? God.
2. What was something Simeon thanked God for? Simeon thanked God for keeping His promise to let him see Jesus before he died. He was so happy to know that the time had come for God to save His people through Jesus.

For You and Me:
Like Simeon, we can thank God for sending Jesus to save sinners, like you and me.

Detective Dan's Lesson #5 Listening Assignment:
1. Why was Simeon so happy to see baby Jesus? He knew that the time had come for God to save God's people from their sins through Jesus.
2. What did God send Jesus to do? God sent Jesus to show us what He's like. And, to take the punishment for the sins of God's people so they could know God and be His people forever.

For You and Me:
God can show us what He's like through His Son, Jesus. Jesus can save us from our sins and make us God's people, too, when we repent of our sins and trust in Him as our Savior.

The Gospel (story wrap-up if NOT using Listening Assignments)

Our Bible Truth is:
How Can I Know What God Is Like?
He Shows Me What He's Like!

God showed Simeon what He is like and He can show us, too! We can ask Him to work in our heart and help us to turn away from disobeying Him and trust in Jesus as our Savior. When we do, God will forgive our sins and save us! He will live in our heart, helping us to know Him right now. He can satisfy our heart, giving us a special kind of happiness that only He can give. And one day, we will go to live with Him in heaven forever. That will be best of all!

Close in prayer.

Closing Unit 1 ACTS Prayer

A=Adoration C=Confession T=Thanksgiving S=Supplication

A　We praise you, God. You show us what You are like!

C　LORD, in our heart we know that You are God. We know we should obey You. but many times we don't want to. Please forgive us. We need a Savior!

T　Thank You for wanting us to know You. Thank You for giving us a heart to know You; and, for making this world that shows us what You are like. Thank You for what we learn about You in Your Word, the Bible. And most of all, thank You for showing us what You are like in Your Son, Jesus.

S　Work deep inside our heart. Help us to turn away from our sins and trust in Jesus as our Savior. Help us to know You. Put in our hearts the special kind of happy only You can give. Help us to go and tell others what we've learned.

In Jesus' name we pray. Amen.

Return to page 7 of the Lesson Plan
for the script of the rest of this lesson.

14

How can I know what God is like?

BIG QUESTION 1

ANSWER:

He shows me what He's like!

The Big Question

Hold up the Big Question sign for all the children to see, and say:

The Big Question we are investigating today is Big Question Number 1:

How Can I Know What God Is Like?
and the Answer is:
He Shows Me What He's Like!

Meaning:
God made us. He wants us to know what He is like so we can know Him, love Him, and praise Him.

God shows us what He is like by the heart He gave us to know and love Him; through all of His creations we see around us; through His Word, the Bible; and most of all, through His very own Son, Jesus Christ.

Let's sing our Big Question Song:"

Big Q & A I Song

HSK ESV Songs 1, track 12
(adapted version of "This Is the Way We Wash Our Clothes")

How can I know what God is like,
God is like, God is like?
How can I know what God is like?
He shows me what He's like!

Place verse in HSK Bible Folder

take out of BQB

HSK Bible Folder

The LORD!

"He who declares to man His thought. The LORD, the God of hosts, is His name." Amos 4:13, ESV

HSK – Bible Verse Picture – front

Unit I Bible Verse

"Who would like to get our Bible verse out of the Big Question Briefcase for me?"

Choose a child to open the briefcase, take out the "Bible" with the Bible Verse in it and hand it to you. Remove the Bible Verse Picture from the "Bible" (held in place by velcro) and hold it up for all the children to see, then say:

Amos 4:13

"He who declares to man what is His thought...The LORD, the God of hosts, is His name."

Meaning:

God wants us to know what He is like so we can know Him, love Him, and praise Him. We don't have to figure out what God is like by ourselves. God show us what He's like--He declares His thoughts to us.

God shows us what He's like through the spirit He put in our hearts; through His creations we see around us; through His Word, the Bible; and most of all, through His very own Son, Jesus Christ.

And what's the name of the one and only true, living God? It's the LORD! Yes, the LORD is His name!

He Who Declares His Thought:
Amos 4:13

"We've said our Bible verse, now let's sing it!"

HSK ESV Songs 1, track 14, 14T

He who declares His thought,
He who declares His thought,
He who declares His thought to man.
He who declares His thought,
He who declares His thought,
He who declares His thought to man.
The LORD, the LORD, is His name.
The LORD, the LORD, is His name.
Amos Four, thirteen.

"Now it's time to do a bit more deep down investigating. Let's read Detective Dan wants us to help him figure out. Would someone like to get it out for me?"

Detective Dan's Listening Assignment #1

VISUAL AID #3

Place verse in HSK Bible Folder

take out of BQB

HSK Bible Folder

#1

Detective Dan's Listening Assignment #1

Hi, Hide 'n' Seek Kids!

I'm working on a brand-new case called:

"The Case of the Old Man Who Looked for God."

I need to find out:

I. Who was the old man who looked for God?

AND

2. How did he find out what God was like?

Can you help me? Listen carefully to the story and you might just hear the answers!

Thanks!

Detective Dan

Then say, "Ok, Hide 'n' Seekers! Put on your best listening ears and see if you can find the answers to Detective Dan's questions. When I finish telling the story, we will see if we can answer all of his questions."

Read the Bible Truth story, putting up the storyboard pictures as you tell it. At the end of the story, repeat the questions and lead the children in answering them. Present the gospel and close in prayer.

Answers to assignment questions, the gospel and ACTS prayer are also included at the end of the story text.

Answers:

1. Who was the old man who looked for God?
Simeon.

2. How did he find out what God was like?
He knew God in his heart; he saw what God was like as he looked around him at the things God had made; he learned about Him in the Bible, God's Word; and most of all, he knew what God was like through His Son, Jesus.

For You and Me:
Like Simeon, we can know what God is like. God has given us a heart to know and love Him. We can look around us and see what He's like in the things He has made. We can learn about Him in the Bible; and, we can know what He's like most of all when we learn about Jesus. We can ask God to show us what He's like and help us to know and love Him. He delights to do this!

Detective Dan's Listening Assignment #2

Detective Dan's
Listening Assignment #2

Hi, Hide 'n' Seek Kids!

I'm still working on the case called:
"The Case of the Old Man Who Looked for God."

Our Bible verse is Amos 4:13: "He who declares to man what is His thought...The LORD, the God of hosts, is His name."

I need to find out:

1. Who did the LORD declare His thought to?

AND

2. What book did the Lord use to declare His thought?

Can you help me? Listen carefully to the story and you might just hear the answers!

Thanks for your help!
Detective Dan

Then say, *"Ok, Hide 'n' Seekers! Put on your best listening ears and see if you can find the answers to Detective Dan's questions. When I finish telling the story, we will see if we can answer all of his questions."*

Read the Bible Truth story, putting up the storyboard pictures as you tell it. At the end of the story, repeat the questions and lead the children in answering them. Present the gospel and close in prayer.

Answers to assignment questions, the gospel and ACTS prayer are also included at the end of the story text.

Answers:

Our Bible Verse is: Amos 4:13
"He who declares to man what is His thought...The LORD, the God of hosts, is His name."

1. Who did the LORD declare His thought to?
Simeon.

2. What book did the Lord use to declare His thought? The Bible, God's Word.

For You and Me:
The LORD can show us what He's like as we look around at all the amazing things He has made. He can declare His thoughts to us as we read the Bible, His Word and learn about His Son, Jesus Ask God to show Himself to you! He delights to do this!

Detective Dan's Listening Assignment #3

Detective Dan's
Listening Assignment #3

#3

Hi, Hide 'n' Seek Kids!

I'm still working on the case called:

"The Case of the Old Man Who Looked for God."

I found four clues, but one of them is NOT in the story. They are: baby Jesus, a chair, God's Word (on a scroll, like in Bible times) and a heart.

Hold up each of the four pictures for the children to see as you identify them. Better yet, put them up on your flannelgraph board, off to one side.

I need to Know:

1. Which THREE pictures belong in the story and which ONE does NOT?

2. What did God use three of these things to show Simeon?

Can you help me? Listen carefully to the story and you might just hear the answers!

Thanks!
Detective Dan

Then say, "Ok, Hide 'n' Seekers! Put on your best listening ears and see if you can find the answers to Detective Dan's questions. When I finish telling the story, we will see if we can answer all of his questions."

Read the Bible Truth story, putting up the storyboard pictures as you tell it. At the end of the story, repeat the questions and lead the children in answering them. Present the gospel and close in prayer.

*Answers to assignment questions, the gospel and ACTS prayer are also included at the end of the story text.**

Answers:

1. Which three pictures belong in the story and which one does not? The chair does not belong.

2. What did God use three of these things to show Simeon? God used baby Jesus, the Bible and the heart He gave Simeon to show Simeon what He is like.

For You and Me:

The LORD wants to show us what He's like, too. He can use the heart He's given us, the Bible, and Jesus to show us what He's like, too.

Baby Jesus

Chair

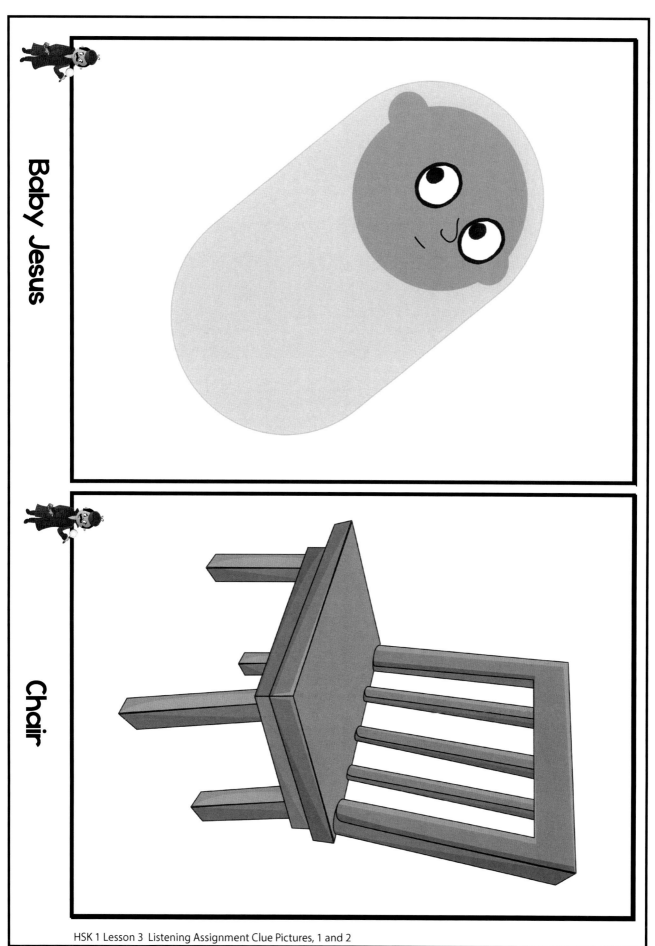

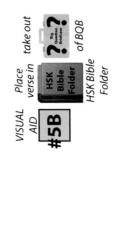

HSK 1 Lesson 3 Listening Assignment Clue Picture1 for kids

HSK 1 Lesson 3 Listening Assignment Clue Picture 2 for kids

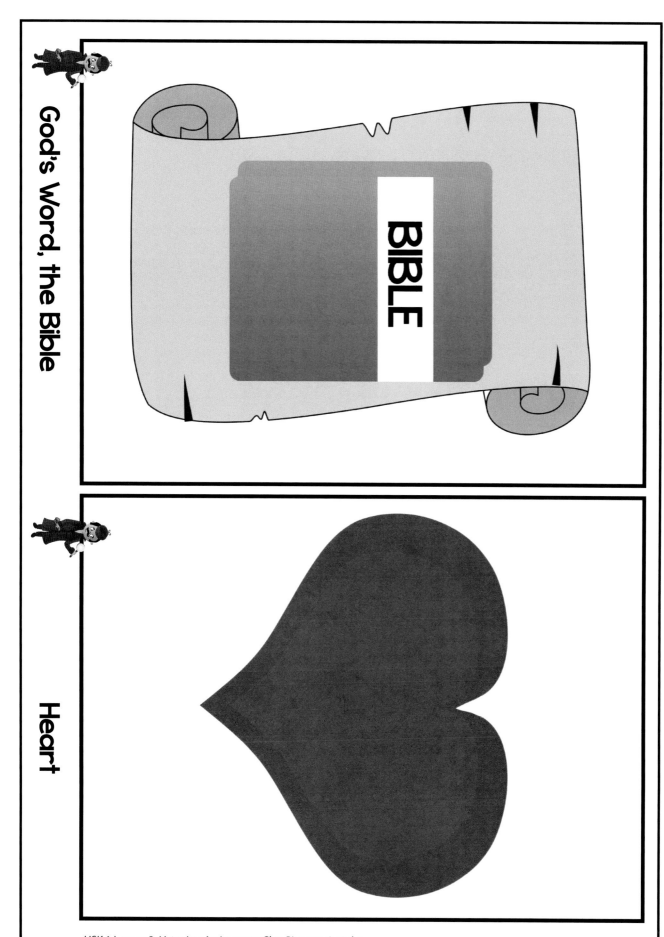

God's Word, the Bible

BIBLE

Heart

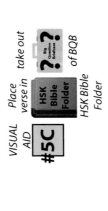

VISUAL AID **#5C**

Place verse in

take out

HSK Bible Folder

Big Question Briefcase

of BQB

HSK 4 Lesson 3 Listening Assignment Clue Picture 3 for kids

VISUAL AID **#5C**

Place verse in

take out

HSK Bible Folder

Big Question Briefcase

of BQB

HSK 4 Lesson 3 Listening Assignment Clue Picture 4 for kids

VISUAL AID #6

Place verse in HSK Bible Folder

take out ?? Big Question BrainCase of BQB

Detective Dan's Listening Assignment #4

Detective Dan's
Listening Assignment #4

#4

Hi, Hide 'n' Seek Kids!

I'm still working on the case called:

"The Case of the Old Man Who Looked for God."

I need to find out:

1. Who did Simeon want to know more and more?
AND
2. What was something Simeon thanked God for?

Can you help me? Listen carefully to the story and you might just hear the answers!

Thanks!
Detective Dan

Then say, "Ok, Hide 'n' Seekers! Put on your best listening ears and see if you can find the answers to Detective Dan's questions. When I finish telling the story, we will see if we can answer all of his questions."

Read the Bible Truth story, putting up the storyboard pictures as you tell it. At the end of the story, repeat the questions and lead the children in answering them. Present the gospel and close in prayer.

Answers to assignment questions, the gospel and ACTS prayer are also included at the end of the story text.

Answers:

1. Who did Simeon want to know more and more about? God.
2. What was something Simeon thanked God for? Simeon thanked God for keeping His promise to let him see Jesus before he died. He was so happy to know that the time had come for God to save His people through Jesus.

For You and Me:
Like Simeon, we can thank God for sending Jesus to save sinners, like you and me.

VISUAL AID
#7

Place verse in

HSK Bible Folder

take out

of BQB

HSK Bible Folder

Detective Dan's Listening Assignment #5

Detective Dan's
Listening Assignment #5

#5

Hi, Hide 'n' Seek Kids!

I'm still working on the case called:
"The Case of the Old Man Who Looked for God."

I need to find out:
1. Why was Simeon so happy to see baby Jesus?
AND
2. What did God send Jesus to do?

Can you help me? Listen carefully to the story and you might just hear the answers!

Thanks!
Detective Dan

Then say, "Ok, Hide 'n' Seekers! Put on your best listening ears and see if you can find the answers to Detective Dan's questions. When I finish telling the story, we will see if we can answer all of his questions."

Read the Bible Truth story, putting up the storyboard pictures as you tell it. At the end of the story, repeat the questions and lead the children in answering them. Present the gospel and close in prayer.

Answers to assignment questions, the gospel and ACTS prayer are also included at the end of the story text.

Answers:

1. Why was Simeon so happy to see baby Jesus? He knew that the time had come for God to save God's people from their sins through Jesus.
2. What did God send Jesus to do? God sent Jesus to show us what He's like. And, to take the punishment for the sins of God's people so they could know God and be His people forever.

For You and Me:
God can show us what He's like through His Son, Jesus. Jesus can save us from our sins and make us God's people, too, when we repent of our sins and trust in Him as our Savior.

Put these pictures in place on your storyboard BEFORE you tell your story.

BG1 Mountains

BG2 Temple

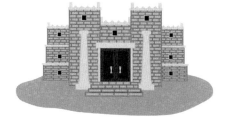

**BG3 Cross/
Resurrection
Scene**

**BG4
Heaven**

HSK I Storyboard Picture Key: Storyboard Pictures (SB)

Store these pictures in numerical order in your HSK Bible Folder.
Add these to your story as you tell it. Numbers correspond to placement order.

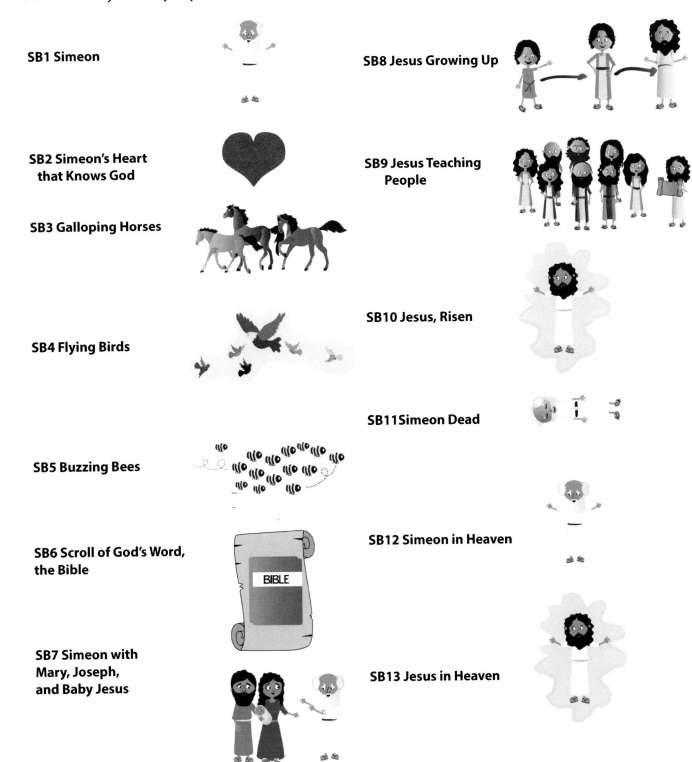

SB1 Simeon

SB2 Simeon's Heart that Knows God

SB3 Galloping Horses

SB4 Flying Birds

SB5 Buzzing Bees

SB6 Scroll of God's Word, the Bible

SB7 Simeon with Mary, Joseph, and Baby Jesus

SB8 Jesus Growing Up

SB9 Jesus Teaching People

SB10 Jesus, Risen

SB11 Simeon Dead

SB12 Simeon in Heaven

SB13 Jesus in Heaven

Note: Use sticky tac putty rather than velcro on back of pictures placed on top of other pictures.

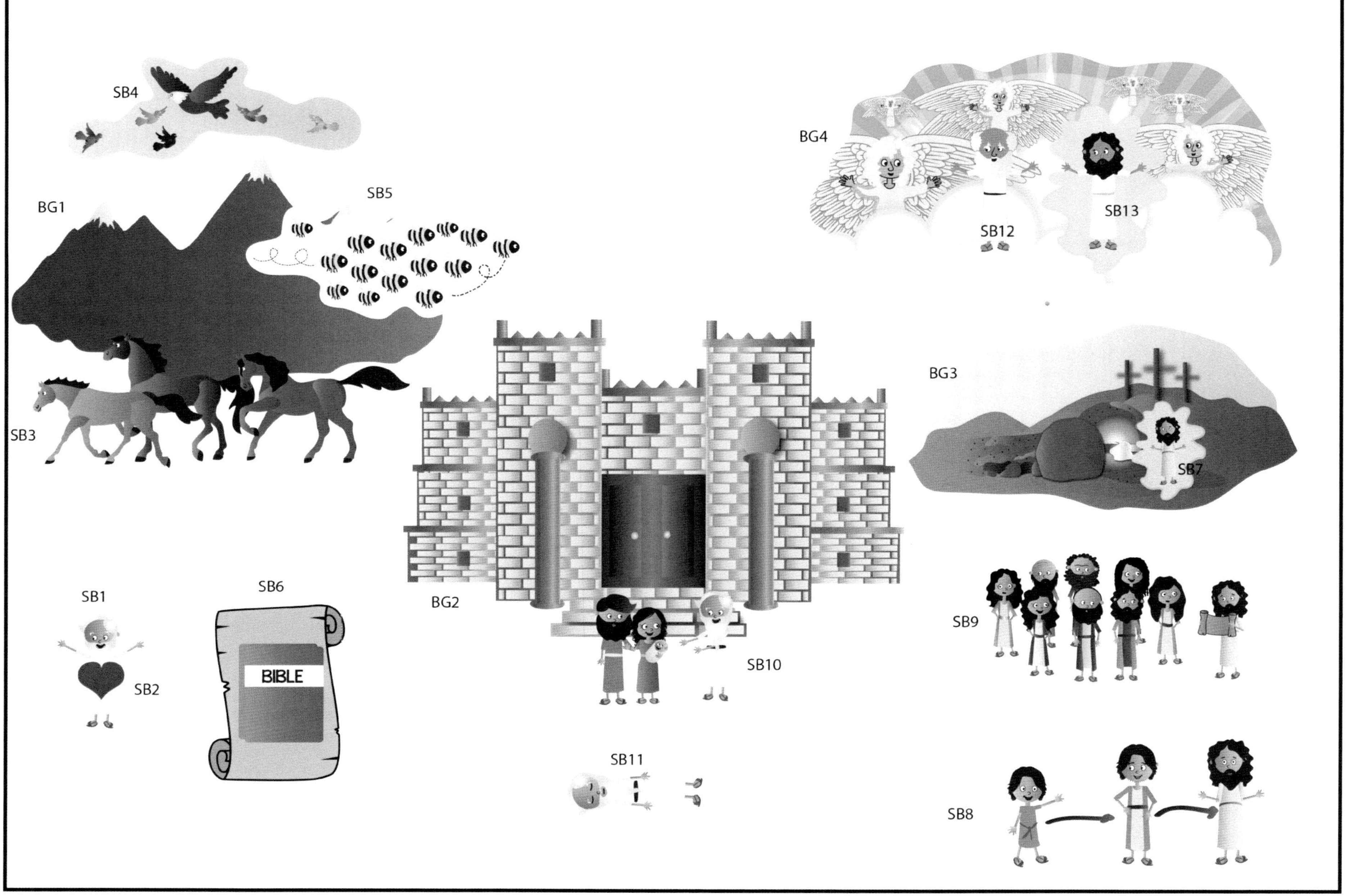

SB13

SB12

BG4

BG3

SB7

SB9

SB8

SB10

SB11

BG2

SB4

SB5

BG1

SB6

BIBLE

SB3

SB1

SB2

HSK I Bible Story: The Old Man Who Looked for God

Suggested Picture Placement

NOTE:
Some of the larger images are assembled from two or more pages. You can make these easier to fold by leaving a small gap in the lamination between the pieces. This allows you to fold the image along the gap.

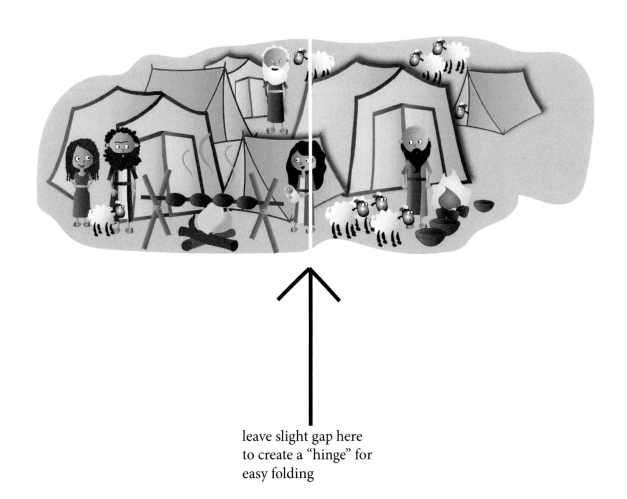

leave slight gap here
to create a "hinge" for
easy folding

BG1 Mountains, pt 1 of 2
HSK 1 Story
glue together, then laminate
Put on board ahead of time

SB13 Jesus in Heaven
HSK 1

BG1 Mountains, pt 2 of 2
HSK 1
glue together, then laminate
Put on board ahead of time

BG4 Heaven pt 1 of 2
HSK 1 Story
glue together, then laminate
Put on board ahead of time

BG4 Heaven pt 2 of 2
HSK 1 Story
glue together, then laminate
Put on board ahead of time

BG2 Temple, pt 1 of 2
HSK 1 Story
glue together, then laminate
Put on board ahead of time

BG2 Temple, pt 2 of 2
HSK 1 Story
glue together, then laminate
Put on board ahead of time

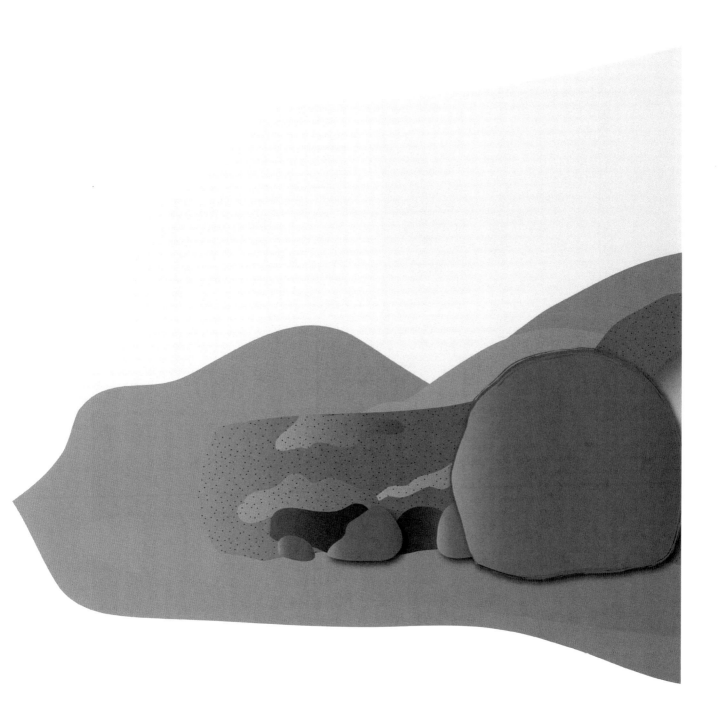

BG3 Cross/Tomb pt 1 of 2
HSK 1 Story
glue together, then laminate
Put on board ahead of time

BG3 Cross/Tomb pt 2 of 2
HSK 1 Story
glue together, then laminate
Put on board ahead of time

SB7 Simeon with
Mary, Joseph and Baby Jesus
HSK 1

SB1 Simeon
HSK 1

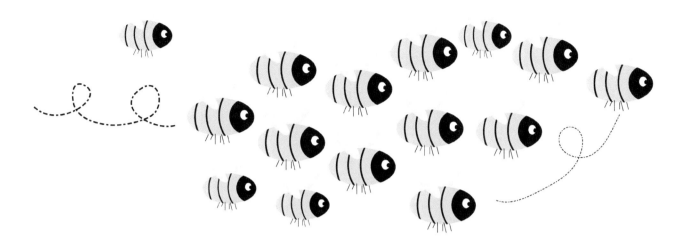

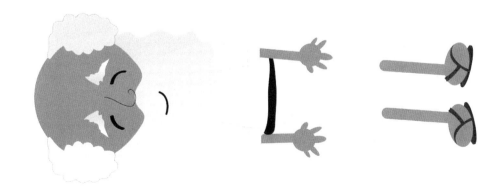

SB5 Buzzing Bees
HSK 1

SB6 The Bible, God's Word
HSK 1

SB11 Simeon Dead
HSK 1

SB10 Jesus Risen
HSK 1

SB12 Simeon in Heaven
HSK 1

SB2 Heart
HSK 1

SB4 Flying Birds
HSK 1

SB3 Galloping Horses
HSK 1

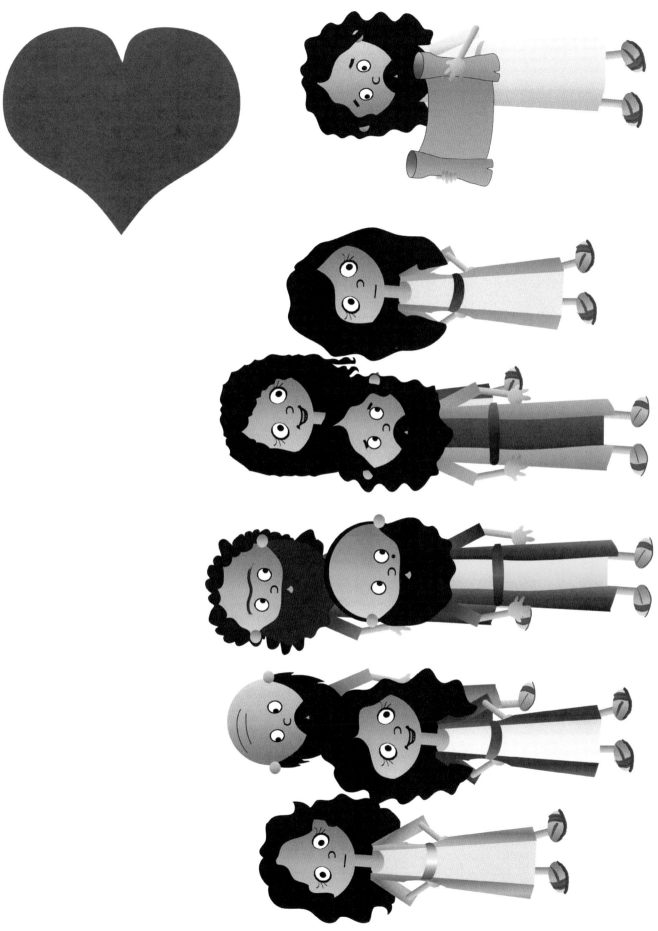

SB9 Jesus Teaching People
HSK 1

SB8 Jesus Growing Up

HSK 1

Hide 'n' Seek Kids

Unit 2
Visual Aids

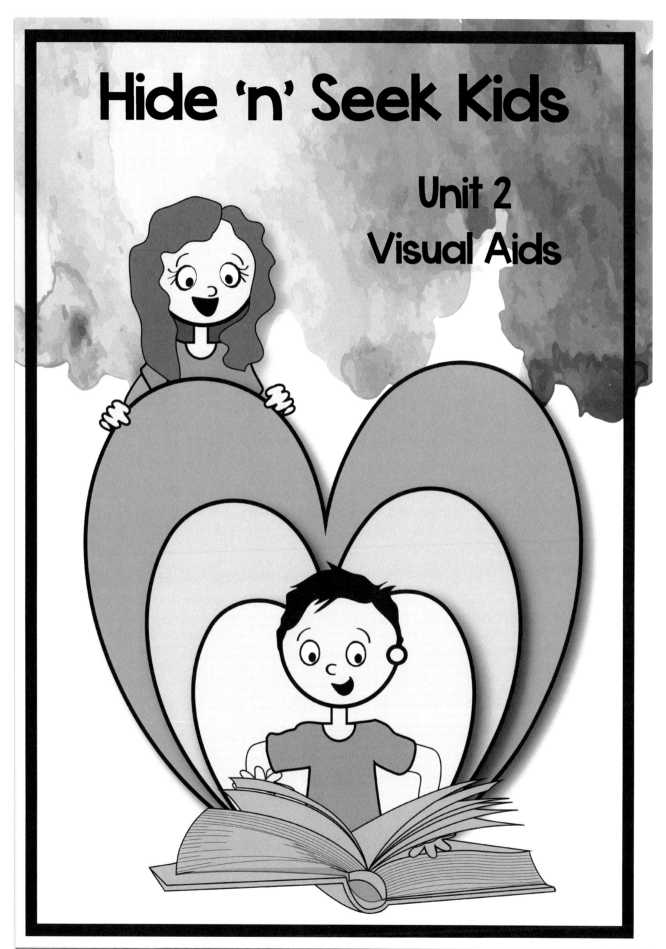

About the Hide 'n' Seek Kids Visual Aids

How Are They Used?

The Hide 'n' Seek Visual Aids book is a companion resource to be used alongside the Hide 'n' Seek Kids Core Curriculum book for each unit. These colorful pictures are used in presenting the key concepts; telling the Bible stories; and, in playing the Bible Story Review games.

What Do They Include?

There are five, different resources included in this book:

1. Key Concept Visual Aids-- colorful signs of the Big Question and Answer, the Bible verse, and the Listening Assignments to use with the 5 lessons for each unit.

2. The Storyboard Picture Key-a who's who of the pictures in thumbnail size. Some pictures are labelled "BG." These are your background pictures that you put on the storyboard before telling the story. The rest of the pictures are labelled "SB." These are pictures you put up on the storyboard as you tell the story.

3. Storyboard Suggested Picture Placement page--where to place the pictures on your storyboard.

4. The pictures, themselves. Notice that each picture is identified and numbered on the back for easy reference. The numbers corrrespond to the numbers in the Picture Placement Key and in the actually story script (found in the Core Curriculum book.)

5. Directions for making the Hide 'n' Seek Kids "Bible" Folder and the **back/front images** to paste in place when making it. (Larger back/front images are found online with the curriculum.)

(Directions for how to make a homemade flannelgraph storyboard and sturdy storyboard pictures are found in **Appendix E in the Core Curriculum book.)**

Ready, Set, Rip It Out!

This book is meant to be ripped up and made into your visual aids. The key concept signs can be cut out and laminated or slipped into sheet protectors. Cut out around the storyboard images and ideally, laminate these. Some of the biggest pictures actually need to be stuck together, before laminating.

Store It!

Hide 'n' Seek Kids is a curriculum that can be used over and over. Store your visual aids and storyboard pictures after using them and they will serve you for many years. We store ours in manilla envelopes and then put them (along with all the rest of the curriculum) in magazine files, labelled by unit. If you have multiple classes using the curriculum, store each set of resources in separate manilla envelopes. This will make prep much simpler, second time around.

Replacement Storyboard Pictures

You can always purchase this book again or simply go online and print out any pictures that go missing.

Two Sizes of Storyboard Pictures

There are two sizes of storyboard pictures to choose from: the standard, large format pictures; or, the smaller format pictures. The larger pictures are best for a big classroom and a storyboard that is at least 36" x 48." (We actually make a whole section of a wall into a felt storyboard!) The small format pictures are created to fit smaller storyboards--in the 24" x 36" to 36" by 48" range. They are most useful in the smaller class or for use at home.

The Case of the Women's Best Gift
  I Timothy

HSK Bible Folder · of BQB

Story-telling Tips

Ahead of time:
1. Read the Bible verses and story. Pray!
2. Choose story action cues and/or prepare storyboard pictures, if using. (Included in Visual Aids book)
3. Practice telling story with the pictures, timing your presentation. Shorten, if necessary to fit your allotted time.

During your presentation:
1. Maintain as much eye contact as possible as you tell the story.
2. Put up storyboard figures/add story action cues as you tell the story. Allow the children to help you put them on the board, if desired.
3. Include the children in your story with a few questions about what they think will happen or words/concepts that might be new to them.
4. Watch the kids for signs that their attention span has been reached. Shorten, if necessary.

INTRODUCTION/ LISTENING ASSIGNMENTS

"Our story is called: The Case of the Women's Best Gift. Here is your listening assignment… "

Read from Detective Dan's Listening Assignment signs, but questions are summarized below:

Detective Dan's Lesson #1 Listening Assignment:

I need to find out:
1. Who are the women in our story?
2. What was their best gift and who did they give it to?

Detective Dan's Lesson #2 Listening Assignment:

Our Bible verse is Psalm 18:30,46: "This God--His ways are perfect. The word of the LORD proves true. The Lord lives, and blessed be my rock, and exalted be the God of my salvation."

As you listen to the story, see if you can figure out:
1. Who in our story knew that God and His Word were perfect?
2. Who did they teach God's Word to?

Detective Dan's Lesson #3 Listening Assignment:
I found four clues, but one of them is NOT in the story.
They are: Food, a zebra, God's Word (on a scroll, like in Bible times) and some clothes.
Hold up each of the four pictures for the children to see as you identify them. Better yet, put them up on your flannelgraph board, off to one side.

I need to know:
1. Which of these things did Grandma Lois and Mother Eunice NOT give to Timothy?
2. Which of these things did they think was most important of all?

Detective Dan's Lesson #4 Listening Assignment:

As you listen to the story, see if you can figure out:
1. Who did Grandma Lois and Mother Eunice want Timothy to know and love most of all?
2. What book did they thank God for giving to them?

Detective Dan's Lesson #5 Listening Assignment:
As you listen to the story, see if you can figure out:
1. What happened in Timothy's heart as he listened to God's Word, the Bible?
2. What good news from the Bible did Timothy preach about when he grew up?

Read the questions, THEN SAY,
"Ok, Hide 'n' Seekers! Put on your best listening ears and see if you can find the answers to Detective Dan's questions. When I finish telling the story, we'll see what we come up with."

"The Case of the Women's Best Gift" I Timothy

Story with lines separating paragraphs (text in bold, optional interaction cues in italics) Numbers correspond to storyboard pictures and placement upon the storyboard. Alway feel free to use less pictures, if it's best for your kids. Simply, black out the numbers next to pictures you do not plan to use. All pictures are found in the Visual Aids book. Put BG (background) pictures on storyboard ahead of time. SB pictures (listed below in story text) are added to board as you tell the story. These numbers are also found on the back of each picture.
Tip: Stack pictures in numerical order before telling story for easy use. Use sticky-back velcro to attach pictures to storyboard felt. Use sticky-tac putty to stick a picture on top of another picture.

(SB1) Grandma Lois and Mother Eunice loved the (SB2) Bible. They loved what the Bible told them about God and His Son, Jesus (SB3). They loved how it worked in their heart(SB4) and helped them know God and live for Him! If Grandma Lois and Mother Eunice knew one thing, it was that there was NO BOOK like the Bible! It alone was God's Word! It was always true. They could count on it.

Do you see a Bible in this room? Point to it.

Now Mother Eunice had a little boy named Timothy (remove BG 1 and show Timothy in BG 2). She and Grandma Lois (SB5) loved Timothy very, very much. And because they loved him, they hugged him… and they fed him good food (SB6)…and they gave him clothes (SB7) to wear…and a good place to sleep at night (SB8). They taught good manners and how to do his chores (SB9) and all sorts of things that would help him grow up to be a fine, young man one day.

Do you have a mother or a grandmother? What kinds of things do they do for you because they love you?

But most of all, because Grandma Lois and Mother Eunice loved Timothy so much, they wanted him to know and love God. And oh, how they wanted Timothy to turn away from his sins and trust in (SB10) Jesus as his Savior one day!

So Grandma Lois and Mother Eunice taught Timothy every day from the only book in the whole, wide world where the truths about God are written down just right. Can you guess what that book is?

Can you guess what that book is called? (I bet you can!) Let's say its name altogether—The Bible!

The Bible, yes, the Bible (SB11) was that one, special book. It alone is God's Word and Grandma Lois and Mother Eunice knew it.

The Bible is a very BIG book filled with so many good stories and so many important truths about God. There was so, so much to teach Timothy!

Hold up your Bible and show the children how big it is. Open it up and show them all the words on the pages.

But of everything in the whole Bible, Grandma Lois and Mother Eunice most wanted Timothy to know one thing.

Can you guess what it is?

They wanted him to know the gospel—the good news of Jesus. They wanted him to know how he could become one of God's people.

"Long ago, God created the whole world, Timothy," they told him. "He gave us his good laws to live by, but we all choose to disobey them, Timothy. " (point to BG3) We need a Savior to save us from our sins and God sent Him to us! It's Jesus!" Grandma Lois and Mother Eunice taught him. "We hope one day you will ask Jesus to forgive your sins and trust in Him as your Savior like we have, Timothy," they told him. "There's nothing better than knowing God and living for Him."

*Story with lines separating paragraphs (**text in bold,** optional interaction cues in italics)*

At first, Timothy just listened and learned as Grandma Lois and Mother Eunice taught him from the Bible. But after a while, something wonderful happened: God's Word began to work powerfully in Timothy's heart and his mind, helping him to believe the gospel.

(SB12) "God, I believe what is written in your word, the Bible. I believe in Your Son, Jesus and trust in Him as my Savior. Please forgive me for disobeying You. I want to live my life for you. Please save me!" Timothy prayed.

God was happy to answer Timothy's prayers. And Timothy was happy to be one of God's people!

Did you know that we can become God's people, too, when we pray like Timothy did, for God to forgive our sins and help us to trust in Jesus as our Savior? It's true!

But that was only the beginning. Now (SB13) Timothy wanted to listen and learn about the Bible (SB14) more than ever! He wanted to know more about God and love Him more, too. And he wanted God's Word to go on working inside his heart, changing him even more.

And that's just what happened! As Timothy kept learning from the Bible, God's Word, it kept on working inside him. And Timothy the little boy grew up and up and up to be Timothy, the man (SB15) with a heart full of love for God, for the Bible, God's Word, and for God's people.

A grown-up man needs a grown up man's job. And what job do you think God gave Timothy to do?

What job do you think Timothy did?

God called Timothy to be a pastor—a man who teaches God's Word to God's people and (SB16) loves them as they gather together at church.

(Remove BG 4 to reveal Timothy in BG 5) Now others gathered around Timothy (SB17) as he preached to them the same truths from the God's Word that Grandma Lois and Mother Eunice had taught him long ago as a little boy!

How happy Grandma Lois and Mother Eunice (SB18) must have been! What a great work God had done in Timothy through His Word, the Bible! And now God was even using Timothy to do a great work in the hearts of others, too!

Let's clap and say, "Yay!" for all the good things God did in Timothy through His Word, the Bible!

Cracking the Case: (story wrap-up for Listening Assignments)

It's time to see how we did with our Listening Assignment.

Detective Dan's Lesson #1 Listening Assignment:
1. Who are the women in our story? Grandma Lois and Mother Eunice.
2. What was their best gift and who did they give it to? Their best gift was teaching God's Word and the good news of Jesus. They taught it to Timothy, Mother Eunice's son.

For You and Me:
Timothy learned God's truths in the Bible and so are you... right now! God used His Word, the Bible, to work in Timothy's heart and help him trust in Jesus as His Savior. He can use His Word to work inside of us, too.

Detective Dan's Lesson #3 Listening Assignment:
I found four clues, but one of them is NOT in the story. They are: Food, a zebra, God's Word (on a scroll, like in Bible times) and some clothes.

1. Which of these things did Grandma Lois and Mother Eunice NOT give to Timothy? The zebra.
2. Which of these things did they think was most important of all? God's Word, the Bible.

For You and Me:
Like Timothy, we have people who love us and who give us many good things. But of everything we can ever have, learning God's Word, the Bible is the most important of all. Ask them to help you learn God's Word.

Detective Dan's Lesson #2 Listening Assignment:
Our Bible verse is Psalm 18:30,46:
"This God--His ways are perfect. The word of the LORD proves true. The Lord lives, and blessed be my rock, and exalted be the God of my salvation."

1. Who in our story knew that God and His Word were perfect? Grandma Lois and Mother Eunice.
2. Who did they teach God's Word to? Timothy.

For You and Me:
God is the living God! He and His Word, the Bible, are still perfect! It will always prove true. We can trust in God and His Word, just like Grandma Lois, Mother Eunice and Timothy did!

Detective Dan's Lesson #4 Listening Assignment:
1. Who did Grandma Lois and Mother Eunice want Timothy to know and love most of all? God.
2. What book did they thank God for giving to them?
The Bible, God's Word.

For You and Me:
God is the best person we can know and love, too. God can use His Word to do wonderful things in our heart, too. Grandma Lois, Mother Eunice and Timothy knew this. Let's thank God for His Word, the Bible. Let's ask Him to use it to do wonderful things in our hearts, too.

Detective Dan's Lesson #5 Listening Assignment:
1. What happened in Timothy's heart as he listened to God's Word, the Bible? God worked in his heart. He turned away from his sins and trust in Jesus as his Savior. Then God kept working in his heart, changing him in wonderful ways, more and more.
2. What good news from the Bible did Timothy preach about when he grew up? God will forgive us our sins and make us His people when we repent and trust in Jesus as our Savior.

For You and Me:
God can use His perfect Word, the Bible, to help us know Him and to change us in wonderful ways. Jesus can save us from our sins and make us God's people, too, when we repent of our sins and trust in Him as our Savior.

The Gospel (story wrap-up if NOT using Listening Assignments)

Our Bible Truth is:
What's So Special about the Bible?
It Alone Is God's Word!

God used His Word, the Bible, to work inside Timothy in wonderful ways. He can work in our hearts, too. We can ask Him to work in our heart and help us to turn away from disobeying Him and trust in Jesus as our Savior. When we do, God will forgive our sins and save us! He will live in our heart, helping us to know Him right now. He can satisfy our heart, giving us a special kind of happiness that only He can give. And one day, we will go to live with Him in heaven forever. That will be best of all!

Close in prayer.

Closing Unit 2 ACTS Prayer

A=Adoration C=Confession T=Thanksgiving S=Supplication

A We praise you, God. You are perfect and everything You tell us always proves true.

C God, we know You are perfect and everything You say is true, but too many times we still don't trust You or obey Your Word. Please forgive us! We need Jesus to be our Savior!

T Thank You for giving us Your words, written down perfectly in the Bible. Thank You that we can always know what is right and true when we read Your Word, the Bible. And thank You for all the wonderful things You tell us about in the Bible, especially the stories about Jesus.

S Work deep inside our hearts. Help us to turn away from our sins and trust in Jesus as our Savior. Help us to want to read Your Word and help us to know You better as we do. Help us to go and tell others how they can learn about You in Your wonderful Word, the Bible.

In Jesus' name we pray. Amen.

What's so special about the Bible?

BIG QUESTION 2

The Bible is God's Word!

ANSWER:

It alone is God's Word!

The Big Question

Hold up the Big Question sign for all the children to see, and say:

The Big Question we are investigating today is Big Question Number 2:

What's So Special about the Bible?
and the Answer is:
It Alone Is God's Word!

Meaning:

There are millions of books in the world, but none is like the Bible. It alone is God's perfect Word! God made sure it was written down just right. It tells us everything we need to know God and how to live for Him. It is powerful to do everything God wants it to do. Everything else in this world may come and go, but God's Word will last forever. It will always prove true.

Let's sing our Big Question Song:"

Big Q & A 2 Song

HSK ESV Songs 2, track 12
(adapted version of "Three, Blind Mice")

What's so special about the Bible?
It alone is God's Word!
It alone is God's Word!
It's always true,
It can make you wise,
It can work pow'rf'ly in your life.
It alone is God's Word!
It alone is God's Word!

"This God—His ways are perfect. The word of the LORD proves true...The Lord lives, and blessed be my rock, and exalted be the God of my salvation." Psalm 18:30,46 ESV

HSK 2 Bible Verse Picture--front

Unit 2 Bible Verse

"Who would like to get our Bible verse out of the Big Question Briefcase for me?"

Choose a child to open the briefcase, take out the "Bible" with the Bible Verse in it and hand it to you. Remove the Bible Verse Picture from the "Bible" (held in place by velcro) and hold it up for all the children to see, then say:

Psalm 18:30,46, ESV

"This God--His ways are perfect. The word of the LORD proves true. The Lord lives, and blessed be my rock, and exalted be the God of my salvation."

Meaning:

The LORD is like no one else. He is the one, true God. Everything He does is absolutely perfect! And, everything He says is perfect, too. It is flawless. Flawless is a big word that means perfect...without even a single mistake. No, not one! God always tells us what is right and true. His Word always proves true!

Where can we read God's Word? In the Bible! It alone is God's Word. That's why we take time each day to learn from the Bible. We want to hear from God--all the wonderful things about Him; what He has done for us through Jesus, His Son; and, what good things are in store for those who love Him and live for Him. Oh, how we want to praise the LORD when we read His Word! He is the living God. He is our Savior!

"We've said our Bible verse, now let's sing it!"

Proves True:
Psalm 18:30

HSK ESV Songs 2, track 14, 14T

This God, His ways are perfect,
The word of the LORD proves true,
This God, His ways are perfect,
The word of the LORD proves true.

This God, His ways are perfect,
The word of the LORD proves true,
This God, His ways are perfect,
The word of the LORD proves true.

Psalm Eighteen, thirty.

"Now it's time to do a bit more deep down investigating. Let's read Detective Dan wants us to help him figure out. Would someone like to get it out for me?"

VISUAL AID #3

Place verse in HSK Bible Folder

take out of BQB

Detective Dan's Listening Assignment #1

Detective Dan's
Listening Assignment #1

Hi, Hide 'n' Seek Kids!

I'm working on a brand-new case called:
"The Case of the Women's Best Gift."

I need to find out:
1. Who are the women in our story?
2. What was their best gift and who did they give it to?

Can you help me? Listen carefully to the story and you might just hear the answers!

Thanks!
Detective Dan

Then say, "Ok, Hide 'n' Seekers! Put on your best listening ears and see if you can find the answers to Detective Dan's questions. When I finish telling the story, we will see if we can answer all of his questions."

Read the Bible Truth story, putting up the storyboard pictures as you tell it. At the end of the story, repeat the questions and lead the children in answering them. Present the gospel and close in prayer.

Answers to assignment questions, the gospel and ACTS prayer are also included at the end of the story text.

Answers:
1. Who are the women in our story? Grandma Lois and Mother Eunice.
2. What was their best gift and who did they give it to? Their best gift was teaching God's Word and the good news of Jesus. They taught it to Timothy, Mother Eunice's son.

For You and Me:
Timothy learned God's truths in the Bible and so are you... right now! God used His Word, the Bible, to work in Timothy's heart and help him trust in Jesus as His Savior. He can use His Word to work inside of us, too.

Place
verse in
HSK Bible
Folder

take out
of BQB

HSK Bible
Folder

#2

Detective Dan's
Listening
Assignment #2

Detective Dan's
Listening Assignment #2

Hi, Hide 'n' Seek Kids!

I'm still working on the case called:

"The Case of the Women's Best Gift."

Our Bible verse is Psalm 18:30,46:

"This God--His ways are perfect. The word of the LORD proves true. The Lord lives, and blessed be my rock, and exalted be the God of my salvation."

I need to find out:

1. Who in our story knew that God and His Word were perfect?

AND

2. Who did they teach God's Word to?

Can you help me? Listen carefully to the story and you might just hear the answers!

Thanks for your help!

Detective Dan

Then say, "Ok, Hide 'n' Seekers! Put on your best listening ears and see if you can find the answers to Detective Dan's questions. When I finish telling the story, we will see if we can answer all of his questions."

Read the Bible Truth story, putting up the storyboard pictures as you tell it. At the end of the story, repeat the questions and lead the children in answering them. Present the gospel and close in prayer.

Answers to assignment questions, the gospel and ACTS prayer are also included at the end of the story text.

Answers:

Our Bible verse is Psalm 18:30,46:

"This God--His ways are perfect. The word of the LORD proves true. The Lord lives, and blessed be my rock, and exalted be the God of my salvation."

1. Who in our story knew that God and His Word were perfect? Grandma Lois and Mother Eunice.

2. Who did they teach God's Word to? Timothy.

For You and Me:

God is the living God! He and His Word, the Bible, are still perfect! It will always prove true. We can trust in God and His Word, just like Grandma Lois, Mother Eunice and Timothy did!

Detective Dan's Listening Assignment #3

#3

Hi, Hide 'n' Seek Kids!

I'm still working on the case called:

"The Case of the Women's Best Gift."

I found four clues, but one of them is NOT in the story. They are: food, a zebra, God's Word (on a scroll, like in Bible times), and some clothes.

Hold up each of the four pictures for the children to see as you identify them. Better yet, put them up on your flannelgraph board, off to one side.

I need to know:

1. Which of these things did Grandma Lois and Mother Eunice NOT give to Timothy?

2. Which of these things did they think was most important of all?

Can you help me? Listen carefully to the story and you might just hear the answers!

Thanks!

Detective Dan

Then say, "Ok, Hide 'n' Seekers! Put on your best listening ears and see if you can find the answers to Detective Dan's questions. When I finish telling the story, we will see if we can answer all of his questions."

Read the Bible Truth story, putting up the storyboard pictures as you tell it. At the end of the story, repeat the questions and lead the children in answering them. Present the gospel and close in prayer.

Answers to assignment questions, the gospel and ACTS prayer are also included at the end of the story text. *

Answers:

1. Which of these things did Grandma Lois and Mother Eunice NOT give to Timothy? *The zebra.*

2. Which of these things did they think was most important of all? *God's Word, the Bible.*

For You and Me:

Like Timothy, we have people who love us and who give us many good things. But of everything we can ever have, learning God's Word, the Bible is the most important of all. Ask them to help you learn God's Word.

Zebra

God's Word, the Bible

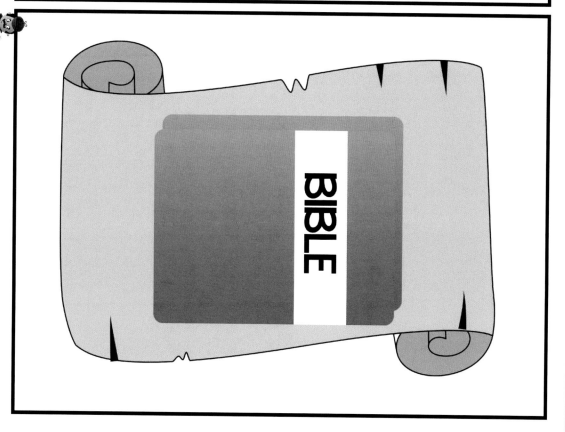

BIBLE

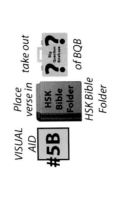

VISUAL AID *Place verse in* *take out*

#5B *HSK Bible Folder* *of BQB*

HSK Bible Folder

HSK 2 Lesson 3 Listening Assignment Clue Picture1 for kids

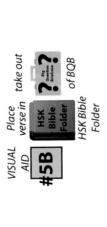

VISUAL AID *Place verse in* *take out*

#5B *HSK Bible Folder* *of BQB*

HSK Bible Folder

HSK 2 Lesson 3 Listening Assignment Clue Picture 2 for kids

Food

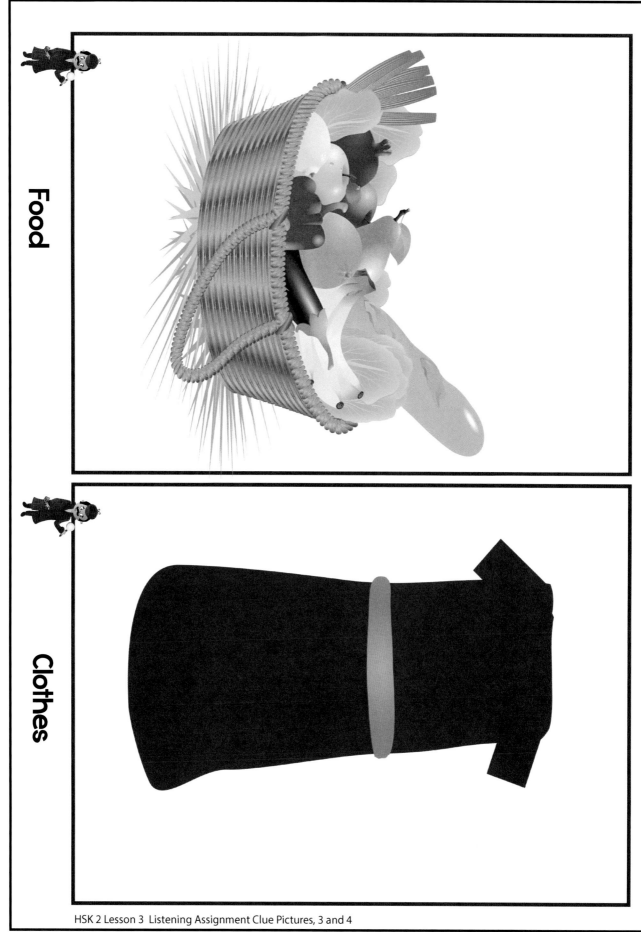

Clothes

HSK 2 Lesson 3 Listening Assignment Clue Pictures, 3 and 4

VISUAL AID **#5C**   *Place verse in*   *take out*

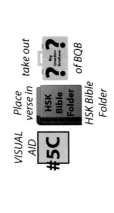

HSK Bible Folder   *of BQB*

HSK 2 Lesson 3 Listening Assignment Clue Picture 3 for kids

VISUAL AID **#5C**   *Place verse in*   *take out*

HSK Bible Folder   *of BQB*

HSK 2 Lesson 3 Listening Assignment Clue Picture 4 for kids

VISUAL
AID

Place
verse in

take out

#6

HSK
Bible
Folder

*HSK Bible
Folder*

Big
Question
Briefcase

of BQB

Detective Dan's
Listening
Assignment #4

Detective Dan's
Listening Assignment #4

Hi, Hide 'n' Seek Kids!

I'm still working on the case called:

"The Case of the Women's Best Gift."

I need to find out:

1. Who did Grandma Lois and Mother Eunice want Timothy to know and love most of all?

AND

2. What book did they thank God for giving to them?

Can you help me? Listen carefully to the story and you might just hear the answers!

Thanks!
Detective Dan

Then say, *"Ok, Hide 'n' Seekers! Put on your best listening ears and see if you can find the answers to Detective Dan's questions. When I finish telling the story, we will see if we can answer all of his questions."*

Read the Bible Truth story, putting up the storyboard pictures as you tell it. At the end of the story, repeat the questions and lead the children in answering them. Present the gospel and close in prayer.

Answers to assignment questions, the gospel and ACTS prayer are also included at the end of the story text.

Answers:

1. Who did Grandma Lois and Mother Eunice want Timothy to know and love most of all? God.

2. What book did they thank God for giving to them? The Bible, God's Word.

For You and Me:

God is the best person we can know and love, too. God can use His Word to do wonderful things in our heart, too. Grandma Lois, Mother Eunice and Timothy knew this. Let's thank God for His Word, the Bible. Let's ask Him to use it to do wonderful things in our hearts, too.

VISUAL AID

**Detective Dan's
Listening
Assignment #5**

Detective Dan's
Listening Assignment #5

Hi, Hide 'n' Seek Kids!

I'm still working on the case called:
"The Case of the Women's Best Gift."

I need to find out:

1. What happened in Timothy's heart as he listened to God's Word, the Bible?

AND

2. What good news from the Bible did Timothy preach about when he grew up?

Can you help me? Listen carefully to the story and you might just hear the answers!

Thanks!
Detective Dan

Read the Bible Truth story, putting up the storyboard pictures as you tell it. At the end of the story, repeat the questions and lead the children in answering them. Present the gospel and close in prayer.

Then say, *"Ok, Hide 'n' Seekers! Put on your best listening ears and see if you can find the answers to Detective Dan's questions. When I finish telling the story, we will see if we can answer all of his questions."*

Answers to assignment questions, the gospel and ACTS prayer are also included at the end of the story text.

Answers:

1. What happened in Timothy's heart as he listened to God's Word, the Bible? God worked in his heart. He turned away from his sins and trust in Jesus as his Savior. Then God kept working in his heart, changing him in wonderful ways, more and more.

2. What good news from the Bible did Timothy preach about when he grew up? God will forgive us our sins and make us His people when we repent and trust in Jesus as our Savior.

For You and Me:
God can use His perfect Word, the Bible, to help us know Him and to change us in wonderful ways. Jesus can save us from our sins and make us God's people, too, when we repent of our sins and trust in Him as our Savior.

HSK 2 Storyboard Picture Key: Background Pictures (BG)

Put these pictures in place on your storyboard BEFORE you tell your story.

BG1 Timothy's Family House--Outside

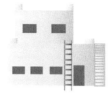

BG2 Timothy's Family House--Inside with Timothy

BG3 Gospel "scene"

BG4 Worship House Outside

BG5 Worship House Inside with Pastor Timothy

HSK 2 Storyboard Picture Key: Storyboard Pictures (SB)

Store these pictures in numerical order in your HSK Bible Folder.
Add these to your story as you tell it. Numbers correspond to placement order.

SB1 Grandma Lois and Mother Eunice

SB11 Learning God's Word

SB2 Bible

SB12 Boy Timothy Praying

SB3 Jesus

SB13 Timothy Happy to Learn about God in the Bible

SB4 Heart

SB14 Wanting to Learn More about God's Word and Jesus

SB5 Grandma Lois and Mother Eunice Love TImothy

SB15 Timothy Grown Up

SB6 Good Food

SB16 Timothy Loving God's People as Their Pastor

SB7 Clothes to Wear

SB17 God's People Gathering to Hear God's Word Preached

SB8 Bed

SB18 Happy Grandma Lois and Mother Eunice

SB9 Chores

SB10 Savior Jesus

Note: Use sticky tac putty rather than velcro on back of pictures placed on top of other pictures.

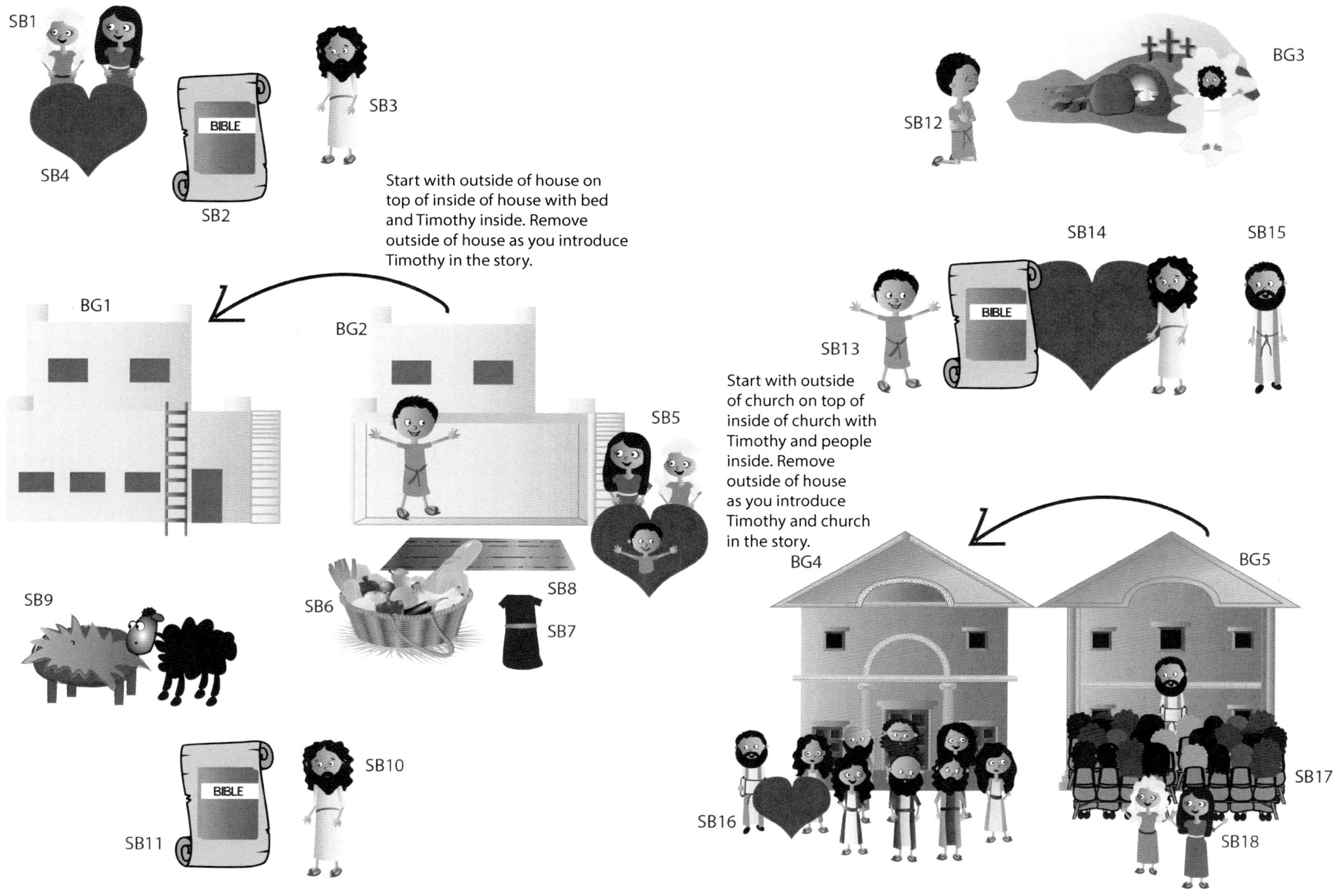

BG3

SB15

SB14

SB12

BIBLE

SB13

SB17

BG5

SB18

Start with outside
of church on top of
inside of church with
Timothy and people
inside. Remove
outside of house
as you introduce
Timothy and church
in the story.

BG4

SB16

SB3

Start with outside of house on
top of inside of house with bed
and Timothy inside. Remove
outside of house as you introduce
Timothy in the story.

SB5

SB8

SB7

BG2

SB2

BIBLE

SB6

SB10

SB1

SB4

BG1

SB9

BIBLE

SB11

HSK 2 Bible Story: The Women's Best Gift

Suggested Picture Placement

NOTE:
Some of the larger images are assembled from two or more pages. You can make these easier to fold by leaving a small gap in the lamination between the pieces. This allows you to fold the image along the gap.

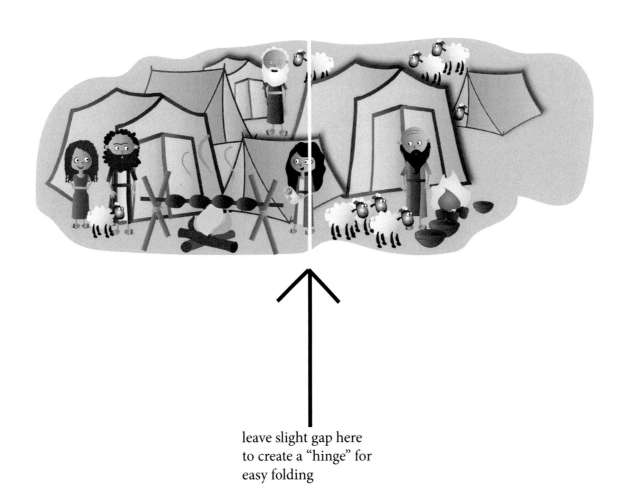

leave slight gap here
to create a "hinge" for
easy folding

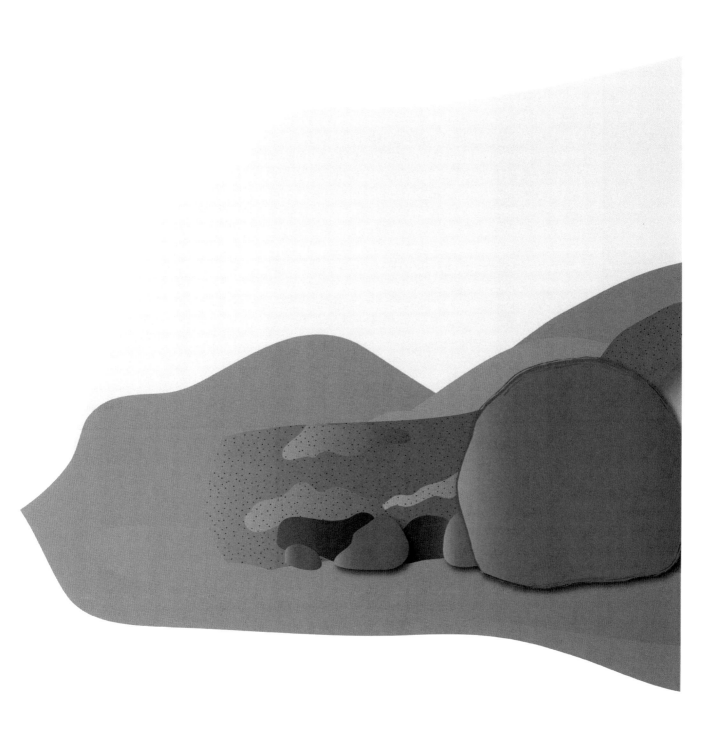

BG3 Gospel Scene pt 1 of 2
HSK 2 Story
glue together, then laminate
Put on board BEFORE telling story

BG3 Gospel Scene pt 2 of 2
HSK 2 Story
glue together, then laminate
Put on board BEFORE telling story

BG 1 Outside of Timothy's House
pg 1 of 2
HSK 2 Story
glue together, then laminate
Put on board BEFORE telling story

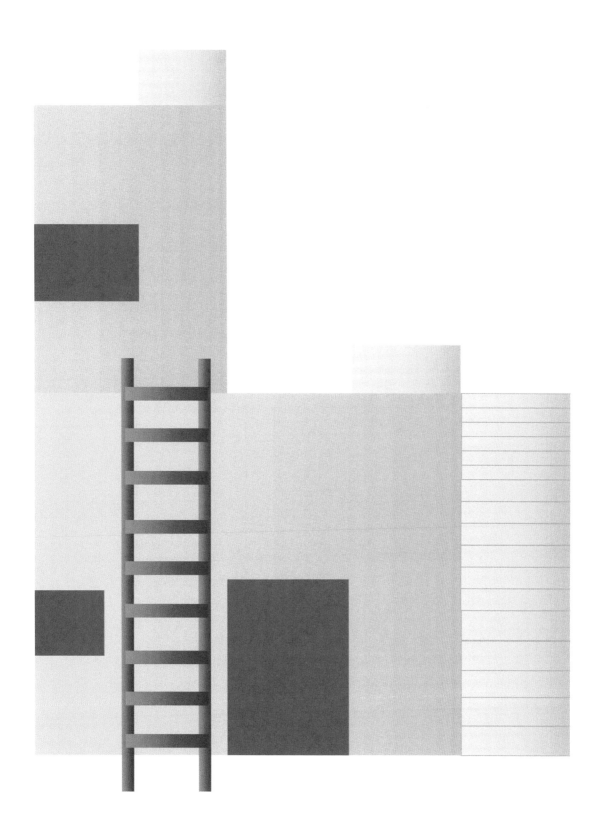

BG 1 Outside of Timothy's House
pg 2 of 2
HSK 2 Story
glue together, then laminate
Put on board BEFORE telling story

BG2 Inside of Timothy's House
pg 1 of 2
Picture 1 HSK 2 Story
glue together, then laminate
Put on board BEFORE telling story

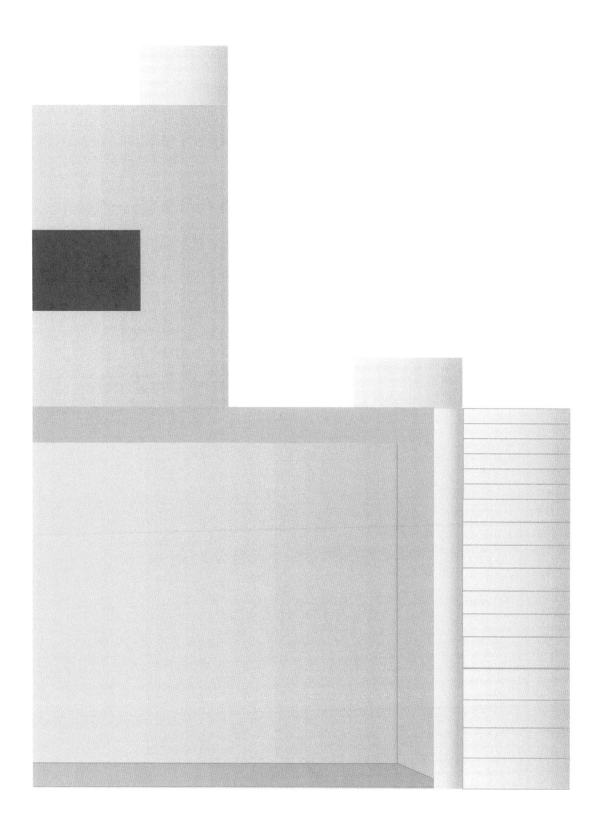

BG2 Inside of Timothy's House
pg 2 of 2
Picture 1 HSK 2 Story
glue together, then laminate
Put on board BEFORE telling story

BG5 Inside of Worship House pg 1 of 2
HSK 2 Story
glue together, then laminate
Put on board BEFORE telling story

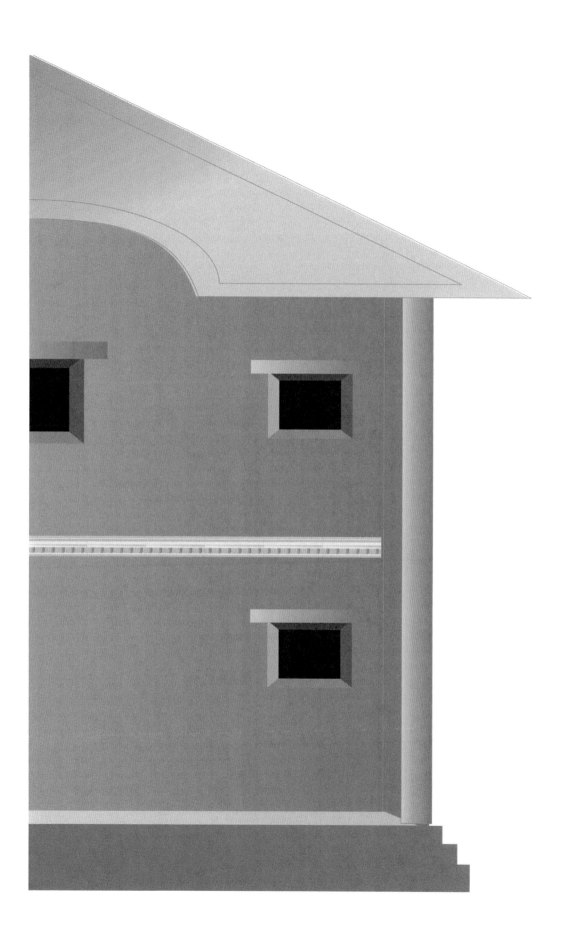

BG5 Inside of Worship House pg 2 of 2
HSK 2 Story
glue together, then laminate
Put on board BEFORE telling story

111

BG4 Outside of Worship House pg 1 of 2
Picture 16 HSK 2 Story
glue together, then laminate
Put on board BEFORE telling story

BG4 Outside of Worship House pg 1 of 2
Picture 16 HSK 2 Story
glue together, then laminate
Put on board BEFORE telling story

SB2 God's Word, the Bible
HSK 2 Story

SB1 Grandma Lois and Mother Eunice
HSK 2 Story

SB11 God's Word, the Bible
HSK 2 Story

SB5 Grandma Lois and Mother Eunice
Love Timothy
HSK 2 Story

SB14 Wanting to Learn More about God's Word and Jesus

HSK 2 Story

SB6 Good Food
HSK 2 Story

SB8 Bed
HSK 2 Story

SB4 Heart
HSK 2 Story

122

SB3 Jesus
HSK 2 Story

SB10 The Savior Jesus
HSK 2 Story

SB9 Timothy's Chores
HSK 2 Story

SB7 Timothy's Clothes to Wear
HSK 2 Story

**SB13 Timothy Happy to Learn
about God in the Bible**
HSK 2 Story

SB18 Grandma Lois and
Mother Eunice Happy,
Praising God
HSK 2 Story

SB12 Timothy Praying
HSK 2 Story

SB15 Grown Up Timothy
HSK 2 Story

SB16 Timothy Loving
God's People
as Their Pastor
HSK 2 Story

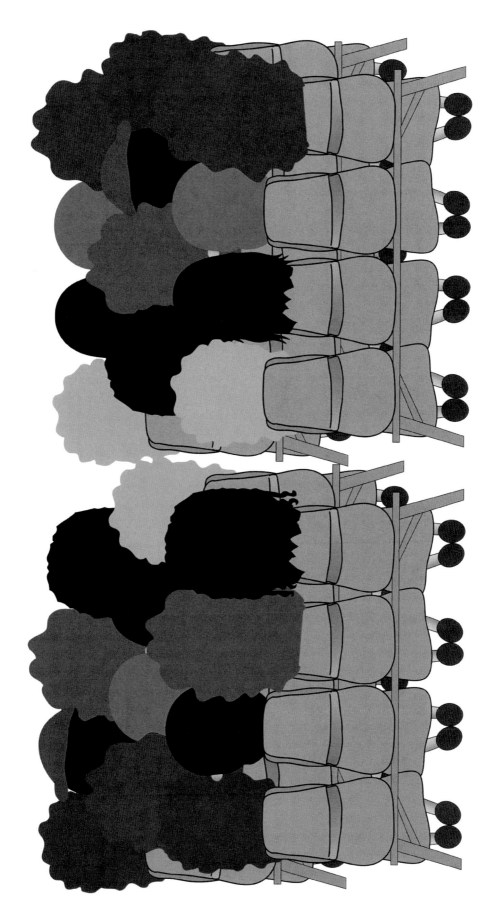

SB17 Timothy Preaching
to Believers Gathered
Together at Church
HSK 2 Story

Hide 'n' Seek Kids

Unit 3
Visual Aids

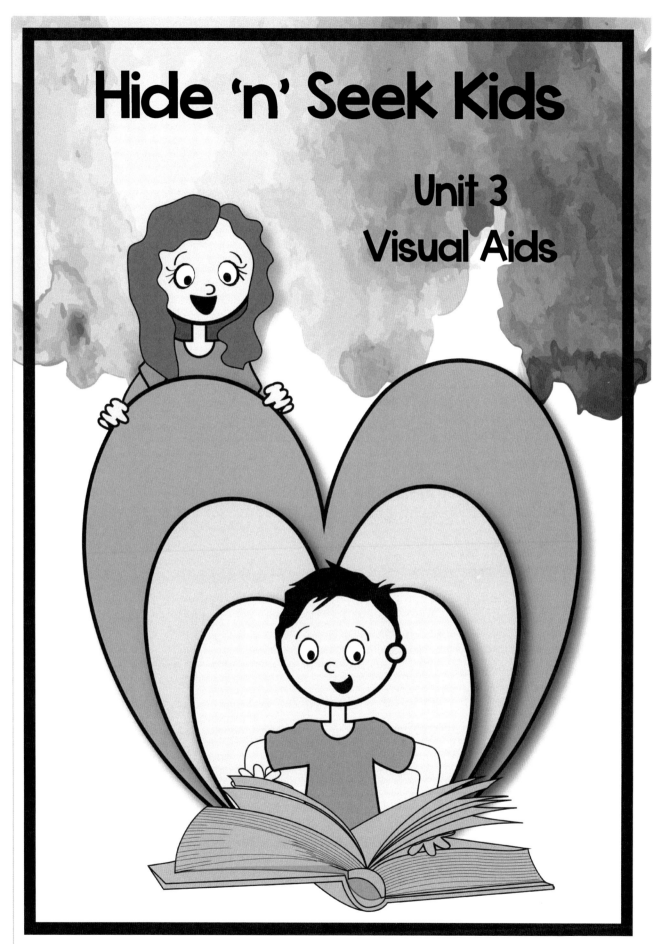

About the Hide 'n' Seek Kids Visual Aids

How Are They Used?

 The Hide 'n' Seek Visual Aids book is a companion resource to be used alongside the Hide 'n' Seek Kids Core Curriculum book for each unit. These colorful pictures are used in presenting the key concepts; telling the Bible stories; and, in playing the Bible Story Review games.

What Do They Include?

 There are five, different resources included in this book:

1. Key Concept Visual Aids-- colorful signs of the Big Question and Answer, the Bible verse, and the Listening Assignments to use with the 5 lessons for each unit.

2. The Storyboard Picture Key-a who's who of the pictures in thumbnail size. Some pictures are labelled "BG." These are your background pictures that you put on the storyboard before telling the story. The rest of the pictures are labelled "SB." These are pictures you put up on the storyboard as you tell the story.

 3. Storyboard Suggested Picture Placement page--where to place the pictures on your storyboard.

4. The pictures, themselves. Notice that each picture is identified and numbered on the back for easy reference. The numbers corrrespond to the numbers in the Picture Placement Key and in the actually story script (found in the Core Curriculum book.)

5. Directions for making the Hide 'n' Seek Kids "Bible" Folder and the **back/front images** to paste in place when making it. (Larger back/front images are found online with the curriculum.)

(Directions for how to make a homemade flannelgraph storyboard and sturdy storyboard pictures are found in **Appendix E in the Core Curriculum book.**)

Ready, Set, Rip It Out!

 This book is meant to be ripped up and made into your visual aids. The key concept signs can be cut out and laminated or slipped into sheet protectors. Cut out around the storyboard images and ideally, laminate these. Some of the biggest pictures actually need to be stuck together, before laminating.

Store It!

 Hide 'n' Seek Kids is a curriculum that can be used over and over. Store your visual aids and storyboard pictures after using them and they will serve you for many years. We store ours in manilla envelopes and then put them (along with all the rest of the curriculum) in magazine files, labelled by unit. If you have multiple classes using the curriculum, store each set of resources in separate manilla envelopes. This will make prep much simpler, second time around.

Replacement Storyboard Pictures

You can always purchase this book again or simply go online and print out any pictures that go missing.

Two Sizes of Storyboard Pictures

There are two sizes of storyboard pictures to choose from: the standard, large format pictures; or, the smaller format pictures. The larger pictures are best for a big classroom and a storyboard that is at least 36" x 48." (We actually make a whole section of a wall into a felt storyboard!) The small format pictures are created to fit smaller storyboards--in the 24" x 36" to 36" by 48" range. They are most useful in the smaller class or for use at home.

The Case of the Stranger's Very Good News
Acts 8:1-8

Story-telling Tips

Ahead of time:
1. Read the Bible verses and story. Pray!
2. Choose story action cues and/or prepare storyboard pictures, if using. (Included in Visual Aids book)
3. Practice telling story with the pictures, timing your presentation. Shorten, if necessary to fit your allotted time.

During your presentation:
1. Maintain as much eye contact as possible as you tell the story.
2. Put up storyboard figures/add story action cues as you tell the story. Allow the children to help you put them on the board, if desired.
3. Include the children in your story with a few questions about what they think will happen or words/concepts that might be new to them.
4. Watch the kids for signs that their attention span has been reached. Shorten, if necessary.

INTRODUCTION/ LISTENING ASSIGNMENTS

"Our story is called: The Case of the Stranger's Very Good News. Here is your listening assignment... "
Read from Detective Dan's Listening Assignment signs, but questions are summarized below:

Detective Dan's Lesson #1 Listening Assignment:

As you listen to the story, see if you can figure out:
1. Who ran away from Jerusalem and went to Samaria?
2. What was the good news he brought with him and shared?

Detective Dan's Lesson #2 Listening Assignment:

Our Bible verse is John 3:16: "For God so loved the world, that he gave his only Son, that whoever believes in him should not perish but have eternal life."

As you listen to the story, see if you can figure out:
1. Who did God use to tell the world the good news about His Son, Jesus?
2. What happened when they shared the good news?

Detective Dan's Lesson #3 Listening Assignment:

I found four clues, but one of them is NOT in the story.
They are: Some enemies; some bags; some sick people; and a horse.
Hold up each of the four pictures for the children to see as you identify them. Better yet, put them up on your flannelgraph board, off to one side.

I need to know:
1. Which three pictures belong in the story and which one does not?
2. How did God use the other three things to spread the good news of Jesus?

Detective Dan's Lesson #4 Listening Assignment:

As you listen to the story, see if you can figure out:
1. Philip told the good news of Jesus to the people of what city?
2. What did they confess to God when they heard the gospel?

Detective Dan's Lesson #5 Listening Assignment:

As you listen to the story, see if you can figure out:
1. Why was it bad news that the Christians had to leave Jerusalem?
2. What good news did they share with people as they ran away to live in new places?

Read the questions, THEN SAY,

"Ok, Hide 'n' Seekers! Put on your best listening ears and see if you can find the answers to Detective Dan's questions. When I finish telling the story, we'll see what we come up with."

"The Case of the Stranger's Very Good News"   Acts 8:1-8

Story with lines separating paragraphs (text in bold, optional interaction cues in italics) Numbers correspond to storyboard pictures and placement upon the storyboard. Alway feel free to use less pictures, if it's best for your kids. Simply, black out the numbers next to pictures you do not plan to use. All pictures are found in the Visual Aids book. Put BG (background) pictures on storyboard ahead of time. SB pictures (listed below in story text) are added to board as you tell the story. These numbers are also found on the back of each picture.
Tip: Stack pictures in numerical order before telling story for easy use. Use sticky-back velcro to attach pictures to storyboard felt. Use sticky-tac putty to stick a picture on top of another picture.

"Run! Pack your bags! Get out of town!" The leaders of the Christians (SB1) told the other Christians (SB2). "Jerusalem isn't safe anymore! The enemies of Jesus (SB3) are after you! They will hurt you and put you in jail if they catch you!" the leaders warned. "So get out of town…NOW!"

How fast would you run if you had enemies trying to get you? Run in place and show me!

That's exactly what most of the Christians did. They (SB4) packed their bags and ran, ran, ran out of town!

Oh, what bad news this was! Or was it? Yes, it was BAD news that these Christians had to leave their homes and their friends and everything they knew in Jerusalem. And it was BAD news that they had enemies who wanted to hurt them. But…. it was GOOD news for the people of the world.

Why? Because when those Christians ran away, they took the gospel (SB5) with them--that wonderful, marvelous, amazing good news about Jesus--and they shared it with everyone they met.

Some of the Christians ran down towards the sea (SB6) and made their home there. And what good news did they tell the people there? The gospel--the good news of Jesus (SB7)!

Some ran towards dry, deserty lands (SB8) and made their home there. And what did they tell the people they met there? The gospel--the good news of Jesus (SB9)!

Some ran towards the tall mountains (SB10) and made their home there.

Can you pretend to climb up a mountain…carrying your bags with you???

And what did they tell the people they met there? The gospel--the good news of Jesus (SB11)!

Some even ran so far away that they went to other countries. One of them was a godly man named Philip (SB12). Philip ran all the way to a place called Samaria and to live. And what did he tell the people he met there?

Can you tell me…the good news of who? Jesus!

You guessed it! The gospel--the good news of Jesus (SB13)!

Story with lines separating paragraphs (text in bold, optional interaction cues in italics)

As (SB14) Philip told the good news of Jesus, crowds of people gathered around and listened. There were poor people and rich people; sick people (SB15) and well people; old people and young people. And to all, Philip told the gospel (SB16), good news of Jesus. This is what he told them:

"God is the good King (SB17) and Creator of the whole world. He created us and we should obey Him. But instead, we've all chosen to disobey Him. Disobeying God is what God calls sin (SB18); and, we deserve His punishment for our sins against Him. We need a Savior!" Philip told them.

"God has sent Jesus (SB19) to be that Savior. Jesus is God's perfect Son who came to earth to suffer and die on the cross to pay for our sins. (SB20) Then, on the third day, Jesus rose from the dead, showing that He had beaten sin and death," Philip shared.

"Now everyone who turns away from sinning and trusts in Jesus as their Savior can be saved. God makes them His people. And they will get to know and live with God forever! This is the gospel—God's good news to you. Come, turn from your sins and trust in Jesus as your Savior today!" Philip told them.

Have you heard this good news before? It is very good news, isn't it?

"What amazing things this stranger is saying," the Samaritans thought! "We haven't heard anything like this before. Could it really be true?" they wondered.

Then God did something marvelous to help them know this good news really was true. Right then and there, Philip prayed for God to heal the sick people listening to him preach. (SB21) And right then and there, without any medicine, or doctor, or hospital, God made them well. By His great power alone!

The people of Samaria were even more amazed! God Holy Spirit (SB22) worked in the hearts of many people as they heard the good news of Jesus and saw God's mighty power to heal the sick. "Surely this good news is true!" they exclaimed. They turned away from their sins and trusted in Jesus as their Savior. They were saved from their sins! God had made them His people!

Let's clap our hands and say, "Yay" for the good things God did in those people!

So, yes, maybe it had been bad news that made Philip run away from Jerusalem. But God had turned that bad news into good news for the people of Samaria. And that made Philip --and them --very, very happy!

Cracking the Case: (story wrap-up for Listening Assignments)	

It's time to see how we did with our Listening Assignment.

Detective Dan's Lesson #1 Listening Assignment:
As you listen to the story, see if you can figure out:
1. Who ran away from Jerusalem and went to Samaria? Philip.
2. What was the good news he brought with him and shared? God forgives our sins and makes us His people when we trust in Jesus as our Savior and live for Him.

For You and Me:
The good news Philip shared wasn't just for the people of Samaria. It's for us, too! God will forgive our sins and make us His people when we trust in Jesus as our Savior and live for Him. God will help us do this, if we ask Him to. What good news that is!

Detective Dan's Lesson #2 Listening Assignment:
Our Bible verse is John 3:16: "For God so loved the world, that he gave his only Son, that whoever believes in him should not perish but have eternal life."

As you listen to the story, see if you can figure out:
1. Who did God use to tell the world the good news about His Son, Jesus? His people--Philip and the other Christians.
2. What happened when they shared the good news? God worked in the hearts of many. They turned from their sins and trusted in Jesus as their Savior.

For You and Me:
God still uses His people today to tell others the good news about His Son, Jesus. God has even used them to tell us the good news of Jesus today! We can ask God to work in our hearts and help us to believe the good news of Jesus. We can ask Him to help us to turn away from our sins and trust in Jesus as our Savior.

Detective Dan's Lesson #3 Listening Assignment:
I found four clues, but one of them is NOT in the story. They are: Some enemies; some bags; another country; and a horse.

1. Which of the three pictures belong in the story and which one does not? The horse does not belong.
2. How did God use the other three things to spread the good news of Jesus? The Christians packed their bags and left Jerusalem to get away from their enemies who wanted to hurt them. They went to live in many places, even other countries, and told the people there the good news of Jesus.

For You and Me:
God has a wonderful plan to tell the whole world the good news of Jesus. He wants everyone to know how their sins can be forgiven and they can become one of His people. And God will use everything as part of this great plan--even very sad things like those believers having to leave them homes. How great is our God! How good and great are His plans!

Detective Dan's Lesson #4 Listening Assignment:
As you listen to the story, see if you can figure out:
1. Philip told the good news of Jesus to the people of what city? The city of Samaria.
2. What did many people confess to God when they heard the gospel? They confessed their sins and asked God to forgive their sins....and He did!

For You and Me:
Like the people of Samaria, we are sinners who need to confess our sins to God. Like them, we can ask Him to forgive our sins... and He can!

Detective Dan's Lesson #5 Listening Assignment:
As you listen to the story, see if you can figure out:
1. Why was it bad news that the Christians had to leave Jerusalem? They had to leave their homes and their friends.
2. What good news did they share with people as they ran away to live in new places? They told them the gospel--how they could become God's people by turning away from their sins and trusting in Jesus as their Savior.

For You and Me:
This good news is for us, too. Jesus can save us from our sins and make us God's people, too, when we repent of our sins and trust in Him as our Savior.

The Gospel (story wrap-up if NOT using Listening Assignments)

Our Bible Truth is:
What Is the Gospel?
It's Salvation through Faith in Jesus Christ!

Philip was so happy when the people of Samaria heard the good news of Jesus and believed. That good news is for us, too! We can ask God to work in our heart and help us to turn away from disobeying Him and trust in Jesus as our Savior. When we do, God will forgive our sins and save us! He will live in our heart, helping us to know Him right now. And one day, we will go to live with Him in heaven forever. That will be best of all!

Close in prayer.

Closing Unit 3 ACTS Prayer

A=Adoration C=Confession T=Thanksgiving S=Supplication

A We praise you, God. You love us so much! You, Yourself, have chosen to send a Savior to save us!

C God, in our hearts we know that You are God and that we should obey You, but many times we don't. We are all sinners who deserve Your punishment for disobeying You. Oh, how we need a Savior!

T Thank You for sending Your dear Son, Jesus to be that Savior. Thank You for making the way for our sins to be forgiven.

S Work deep inside our hearts. Help us to turn away from our sins and trust in Jesus as our Savior. Help us to know You and live for You. Help us to go and tell others the good news of the gospel, too. In Jesus' name we pray.

   In Jesus' name we pray. Amen.

What Is the Gospel?

BIG QUESTION 3

ANSWER:

It's Salvation through Faith in Jesus Christ!

HSK 3 Big Question and Answer Sign Front

The Big Question

Hold up the Big Question sign for all the children to see,

and say:

The Big Question we are investigating today is
Big Question Number 3:

What Is the Gospel?
and the Answer is:

It's Salvation through Faith in Jesus Christ!

Meaning:

Gospel means "good news." In the Bible, the gospel is the good news that God sent His Son, Jesus to save sinners like you and me from the punishment we deserve for our sins. Jesus did this when He suffered and died on the cross, giving His perfect life as the full payment for our sins. This salvation is for all who turn away from their sins and trust in Jesus as their Savior. It is a gift God offers to us, too. Now that is good news, indeed!

Let's sing our Big Question Song:"

Big Q & A 3 Song

HSK ESV Songs 3, track 12

(adapted version of "Oh, My Darlin' Clementine")

What's the gospel?
What's the gospel?
Can you tell me what it is?
It's salvation through faith in Jesus,
That's what the gospel is. (repeat)

"For God so loved the world, that he gave his only Son, that whoever believes in him should not perish but have eternal life." JOHN 3:16

HSK 3 Bible Verse Picture--front

Unit 3 Bible Verse

"Who would like to get our Bible verse out of the Big Question Briefcase for me?"

Choose a child to open the briefcase, take out the "Bible" with the Bible Verse in it and hand it to you. Remove the Bible Verse Picture from the "Bible" (held in place by velcro) and hold it up for all the children to see, then say:

John 3:16

"For God so loved the world, that he gave his only Son, that whoever believes in him should not perish but have eternal life."

Meaning:

How great is God's love for sinners like you and me, that He would send His own, dear Son, Jesus to suffer and die for us! Now all who turn from their sins and trust in Jesus as their Savior will not perish. They will not receive the punishment they deserve for their sins. Jesus has already paid for their sins when He died on the cross. Because of what Jesus has done for them, these people will enjoy eternal life with God. Here on earth, they will know God in their hearts and His care in their lives. And when they die, they will go to be with Him forever! God offers us eternal life, too, when we turn away from our sins and trust in Jesus as our Savior.

"We've said our Bible verse, now let's sing it!"

For God So Loved the World: John 3:16

HSK ESV Songs 3, track 14, 14T

For God so loved the world,
That He gave His only Son,
That whoever believes in Him
Shouldn't perish,
But have eternal life. (refrain)
John Three, sixteen.

"Now it's time to do a bit more deep down investigating. Let's read Detective Dan wants us to help him figure out. Would someone like to get it out for me?"

Detective Dan's Listening Assignment #1

#1

Hi, Hide 'n' Seek Kids!

I'm working on a brand-new case called:

"The Case of the Stranger's Very Good News."

I need to find out:

1. Who ran away from Jerusalem and went to Samaria?

AND

2. What was the good news he brought with him and shared?

Can you help me? Listen carefully to the story and you might just hear the answers!

Thanks!
Detective Dan

Then say, "Ok, Hide 'n' Seekers! Put on your best listening ears and see if you can find the answers to Detective Dan's questions. When I finish telling the story, we will see if we can answer all of his questions."

Read the Bible Truth story, putting up the storyboard pictures as you tell it. At the end of the story, repeat the questions and lead the children in answering them. Present the gospel and close in prayer.

Answers to assignment questions, the gospel and ACTS prayer are also included at the end of the story text.

Answers:

1. Who ran away from Jerusalem and went to Samaria? Philip.

2. What was the good news he brought with him and shared? God forgives our sins and makes us His people when we trust in Jesus as our Savior and live for Him.

For You and Me:

The good news Philip shared wasn't just for the people of Samaria. It's for us, too! God will forgive our sins and make us His people when we trust in Jesus as our Savior and live for Him. God will help us do this, if we ask Him to. What good news that is!

Detective Dan's
Listening Assignment #2

Hi, Hide 'n' Seek Kids!

I'm still working on the case called:

"The Case of the Stranger's Very Good News."

Our Bible verse is John 3:16:

"For God so loved the world, that he gave his only Son, that whoever believes in him should not perish but have eternal life."

I need to find out:

1. Who did God use to tell the world the good news about His Son, Jesus?

AND

2. What happened when they shared the good news?

Can you help me? Listen carefully to the story and you might just hear the answers!

Thanks for your help!

Detective Dan

Then say, "Ok, Hide 'n' Seekers! Put on your best listening ears and see if you can find the answers to Detective Dan's questions. When I finish telling the story, we will see if we can answer all of his questions."

Read the Bible Truth story, putting up the storyboard pictures as you tell it. At the end of the story, repeat the questions and lead the children in answering them. Present the gospel and close in prayer.

Answers to assignment questions, the gospel and ACTS prayer are also included at the end of the story text.

Answers:

Our Bible verse is John 3:16: "For God so loved the world, that he gave his only Son, that whoever believes in him should not perish but have eternal life."

As you listen to the story, see if you can figure out:

1. Who did God use to tell the world the good news about His Son, Jesus? His people--Philip and the other Christians.

2. What happened when they shared the good news? God worked in the hearts of many. They turned from their sins and trusted in Jesus as their Savior.

For You and Me:

God still uses His people today to tell others the good news about His Son, Jesus. God has even used them to tell us the good news of Jesus today! We can ask God to work in our hearts and help us to believe the good news of Jesus. We can ask Him to help us to turn away from our sins and trust in Jesus as our Savior.

VISUAL
AID
#5A

Place
verse in

HSK
Bible
Folder

HSK Bible
Folder

take out

?? Big
Question
Boxes

of BQB

#3

Detective Dan's Listening Assignment #3

Detective Dan's
Listening Assignment #3

Hi, Hide 'n' Seek Kids!
I'm still working on the case called:
"The Case of the Stranger's Very Good News.

I found four clues, but one of them is NOT in the story.
They are: Some enemies; some bags; another country; and a horse.

Hold up each of the four pictures for the children to see as you identify them. Better yet, put them up on your flannelgraph board, off to one side.

I need to know:
1. Which of the three pictures belong in the story and which one does not?
AND
2. How did God use the other three things to spread the good news of Jesus?

Can you help me? Listen carefully to the story and you might just hear the answers!

Thanks!
Detective Dan

Then say, "Ok, Hide'n'Seekers! Put on your best listening ears and see if you can find the answers to Detective Dan's questions. When I finish telling the story, we will see if we can answer all of his questions."

Read the Bible Truth story, putting up the storyboard pictures as you tell it. At the end of the story, repeat the questions and lead the children in answering them. Present the gospel and close in prayer.

Answers to assignment questions, the gospel and ACTS prayer are also included at the end of the story text.

Answers:
1. Which of the three pictures belong in the story and which one does not? The horse does not belong.
2. How did God use the other three things to spread the good news of Jesus? The Christians packed their bags and left Jerusalem to get away from their enemies who wanted to hurt them. They went to live in many places, even other countries, and told the people there the good news of Jesus.

For You and Me:
God has a wonderful plan to tell the whole world the good news of Jesus. He wants everyone to know how their sins can be forgiven and they can become one of His people. And God will use everything as part of this great plan–even very sad things like those believers having to leave their homes. How great is our God! How good and great are His plans!

Enemies

Some Bags

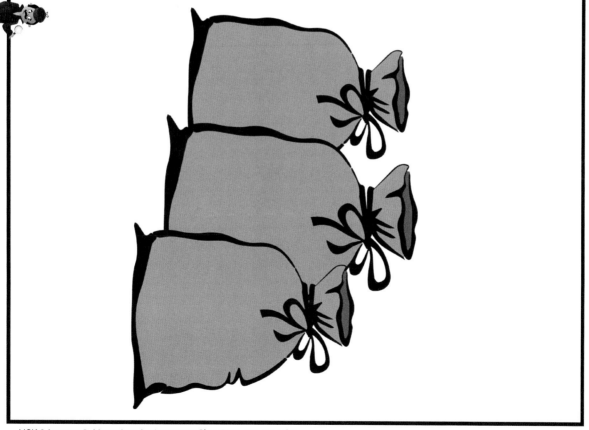

VISUAL *Place* *take out*
AID *verse in*

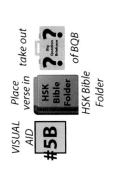

of BQB

HSK Bible
Folder

HSK 3 Lesson 3 Listening Assignment Clue Picture1 for kids

VISUAL *Place* *take out*
AID *verse in*

of BQB

HSK Bible
Folder

HSK 3 Lesson 3 Listening Assignment Clue Picture 2 for kids

Another Country

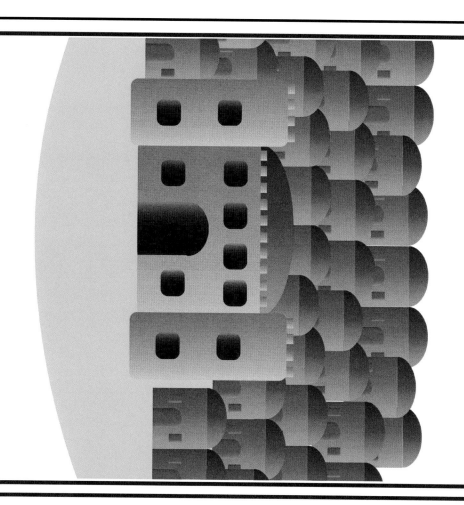

A Horse

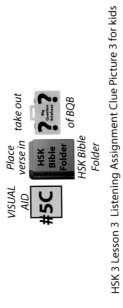

*VISUAL
AID*

*Place
verse in*   *take out*

#5C   HSK
Bible
Folder   Big
Question
Briefcase

*HSK Bible
Folder*   *of BQB*

HSK 3 Lesson 3 Listening Assignment Clue Picture 3 for kids

*VISUAL
AID*

*Place
verse in*   *take out*

#5C   HSK
Bible
Folder   Big
Question
Briefcase

*HSK Bible
Folder*   *of BQB*

HSK 3 Lesson 3 Listening Assignment Clue Picture 4 for kids

Detective Dan's
Listening
Assignment #4

#4

VISUAL
AID
#6

Place
verse in

take out

of BQB

HSK
Bible
Folder

HSK Bible
Folder

Detective Dan's
Listening Assignment #4

#4

Hi, Hide 'n' Seek Kids!

I'm still working on the case called:

"The Case of the Stranger's Very Good News."

I need to find out:

I. Philip told the good news of Jesus to the people of what city?

AND

2. What did many people confess to God when they heard the gospel?

Can you help me? Listen carefully to the story and you might just hear the answers!

Thanks!
Detective Dan

Then say, "Ok, Hide 'n' Seekers! Put on your best listening ears and see if you can find the answers to Detective Dan's questions. When I finish telling the story, we will see if we can answer all of his questions."

Read the Bible Truth story, putting up the storyboard pictures as you tell it. At the end of the story, repeat the questions and lead the children in answering them. Present the gospel and close in prayer.

Answers to assignment questions, the gospel and ACTS prayer are also included at the end of the story text.

Answers:

1. Philip told the good news of Jesus to the people of what city? The city of Samaria.

2. What did many people confess to God when they heard the gospel? They confessed their sins and asked God to forgive their sins...and He did!

For You and Me:
Like the people of Samaria, we are sinners who need to confess our sins to God. Like them, we can ask Him to forgive our sins... and He can!

Detective Dan's Listening Assignment #5

#5

Detective Dan's
Listening Assignment #5

Hi, Hide 'n' Seek Kids!

I'm still working on the case called:
"The Case of the Stranger's Very Good News."

I need to find out:

1. Why was it bad news that the Christians had to leave Jerusalem?

AND

2. What good news did they share with people as they ran away to live in new places?

Can you help me? Listen carefully to the story and you might just hear the answers!

Thanks!
Detective Dan

Then say, *"Ok, Hide 'n' Seekers! Put on your best listening ears and see if you can find the answers to Detective Dan's questions. When I finish telling the story, we will see if we can answer all of his questions."*

Read the Bible Truth story, putting up the storyboard pictures as you tell it. At the end of the story, repeat the questions and lead the children in answering them. Present the gospel and close in prayer.

Answers to assignment questions, the gospel and ACTS prayer are also included at the end of the story text.

Answers:

1. Why was it bad news that the Christians had to leave Jerusalem? They had to leave their homes and their friends.

2. What good news did they share with people as they ran away to live in new places? They told them that they can become God's people when they turn away from their sins and trust in Jesus as their Savior.

For You and Me:
They told them the gospel--how they could become God's people by turning away from their sins and trusting in Jesus as their Savior.

HSK 3 Storyboard Picture Key: Background Pictures (BG)

Put these pictures in place on your storyboard BEFORE you tell your story.

BG1 City of Jerusalem

BG2 Jail

BG3 Homes next to Sea with People

BG4 Homes in Desert with People

BG5 Homes in Mountains with People

BG6 Homes in Other Courntries (Samaria)

BG7 Cross/Tomb Scene

HSK 3 Storyboard Picture Key: Storyboard Pictures (SB)

Store these pictures in numerical order in your HSK Bible Folder.
Add these to your story as you tell it. Numbers correspond to placement order.

SB1 Christian leaders

SB2 Group of Christians

SB3 Enemies of the Christians

SB4 Christians Running to Other Places

SB5 The Gospel

SB6 Believers Who Fled to the Sea

SB7 The Gospel

SB8 Believers Who Fled to the Desert

SB9 The Gospel

SB10 Believers Who Fled to the Mountains

SB11 The Gospel

SB12 Philip

SB13 The Gospel

SB14 Philip Telling the Gospel

SB15 Sick People of Samaria

SB16 The Gospel

SB17 God Is King of the World

SB18 "Sin"

SB19 Jesus Died for the Sins of God's People

SB20 Jesus Rose from the Dead in Victory

SB21 Sick People Healed

SB22 Holy Spirit Working in Hearts

Note: Use sticky tac putty rather than velcro on back of pictures placed on top of other pictures.

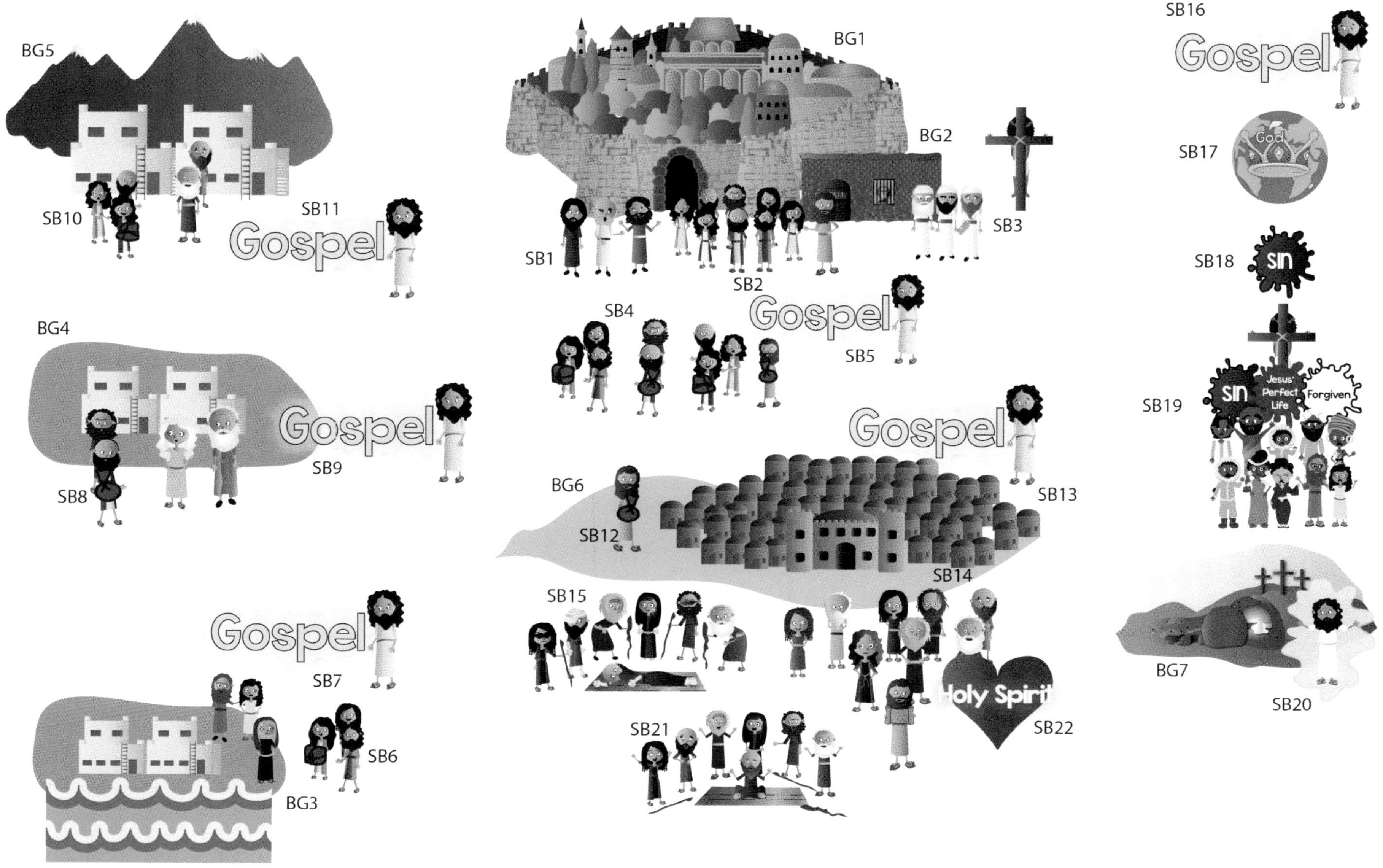

SB16 Gospel

SB17

SB18 Sin

SB19 Sin Jesus Perfect Life Forgiven

BG7 SB20

SB3

BG2

BG1

SB5 Gospel

SB2

SB4

SB1

SB13 Gospel

SB14

SB22 Holy Spirit

BG6

SB12

SB15

SB21

SB11 Gospel

BG5

SB10

SB9 Gospel

BG4

SB8

SB7 Gospel

SB6

BG3

161

Suggested Picture Placement

NOTE:
Some of the larger images are assembled from two or more pages. You can make these easier to fold by leaving a small gap in the lamination between the pieces. This allows you to fold the image along the gap.

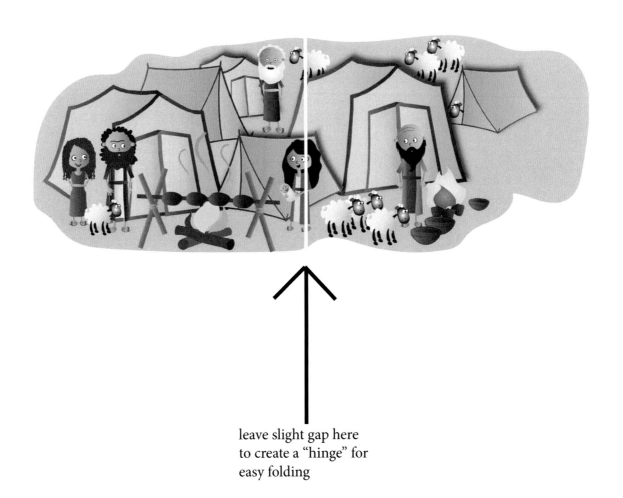

leave slight gap here
to create a "hinge" for
easy folding

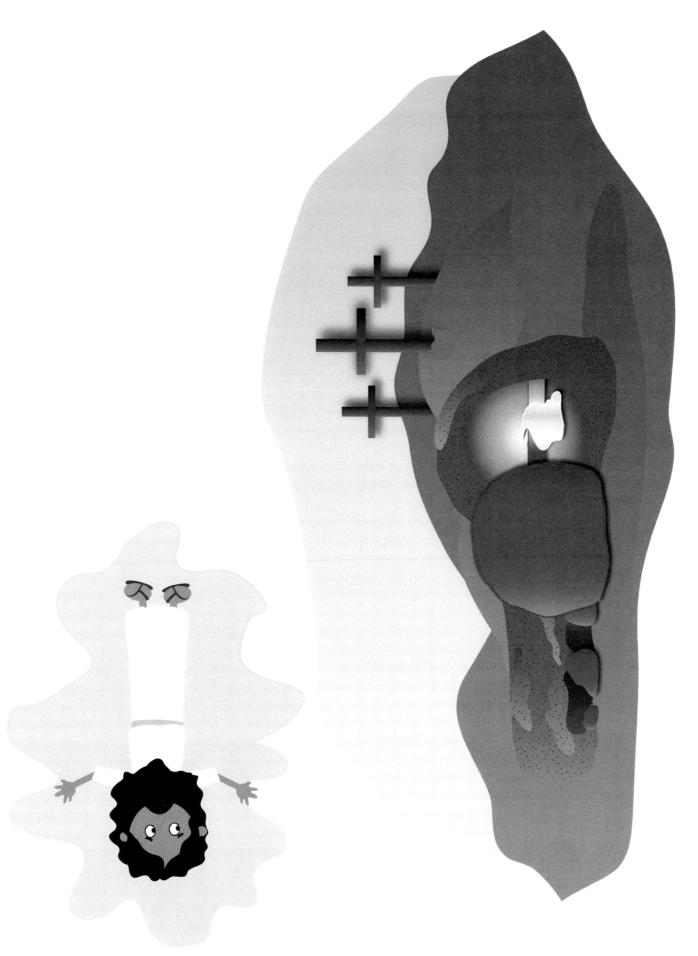

BG7 Cross/Tomb Scene
HSK3
Place on board BEFORE telling story

SB20 Jesus Rose in Victory
HSK3

BG1 Jerusalem pt 1 of 2
HSK 3 Story
glue together, then laminate
Put on board before telling story

BG1 Jerusalem pt 2 of 2
HSK 3 Story
glue together, then laminate
Put on board before telling story

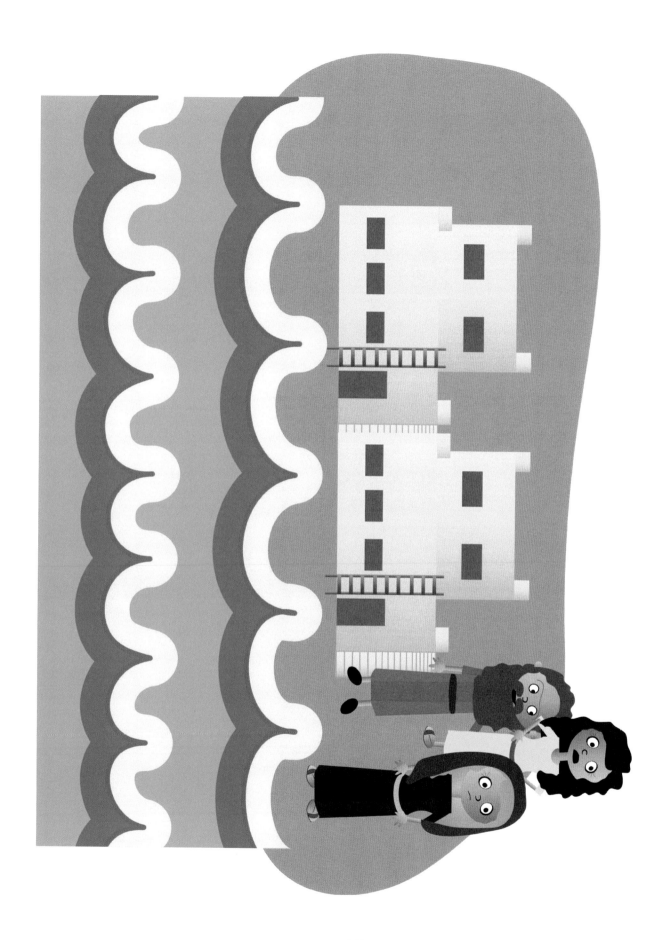

BG 3 Sea City
HSK 3 Story
Put on board before telling story

170

BG 6 Other Country/Samaria pt 1 of 2
HSK 3 Story
glue together, then laminate
Put on board before telling story

BG 6 Other Country/Samaria pt 1 of 2
HSK 3 Story
glue together, then laminate
Put on board before telling story

BG5 Mountain City pt 1 of 2
HSK 3 Story
glue together, then laminate
Put on board before telling story

BG5 Mountain City pt 2 of 2
HSK 3 Story
glue together, then laminate
Put on board before telling story

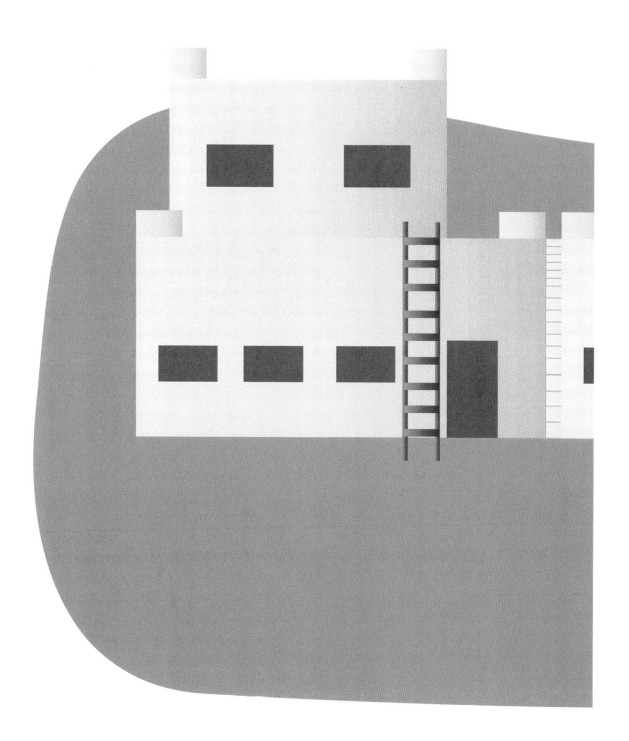

BG4 Desert City pt 1 of 2
HSK 3 Story
glue together, then laminate
Put on board before telling story

BG4 Desert City pt 2 of 2
HSK 3 Story
glue together, then laminate
Put on board before telling story

SB14 Philip Telling the Gospel
HSK 3 Story

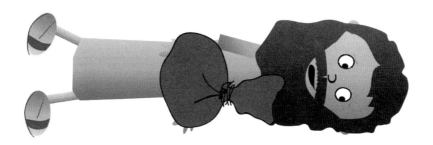

SB19 Jesus Pays for the Sins of God's People
HSK 3 Story

SB12 Philip Goes to Samaria
HSK 3 Story

SB 9 The Gospel
HSK 3 Story

SB5 The Gospel
HSK 3 Story

SB 11 The Gospel
HSK 3 Story

SB 13 The Gospel
HSK 3 Story

SB 7 The Gospel
HSK 3 Story

SB 16 The Gospel
HSK 3 Story

SB15
Sick Samaritans
HSK 3 Story

SB21 Healed
Samaritans
HSK 3 Story

SB1 Christian Leaders
HSK 3 Story

SB4 Believers Leaving Jerusalem
HSK 3 Story

SB6 Believers
Fleeing
to Sea City
HSK 3 Story

SB8 Believers
Fleeing to Desert
City
HSK 3 Story

SB10 Believers
Fleeing to
Mountain City
HSK 3 Story

SB3 Enemies of
the Christians
HSK 3 Story

**SB2 Believers
Listening**
HSK 3 Story

SB18 Sin
HSK 3 Story

**SB22 Holy Spirit Working
in Their Hearts**
HSK 3 Story

BG2 Jail
HSK 3 Story

**SB17 God Is King
of the World**
HSK 3 Story

Hide 'n' Seek Kids

Unit 4
Visual Aids

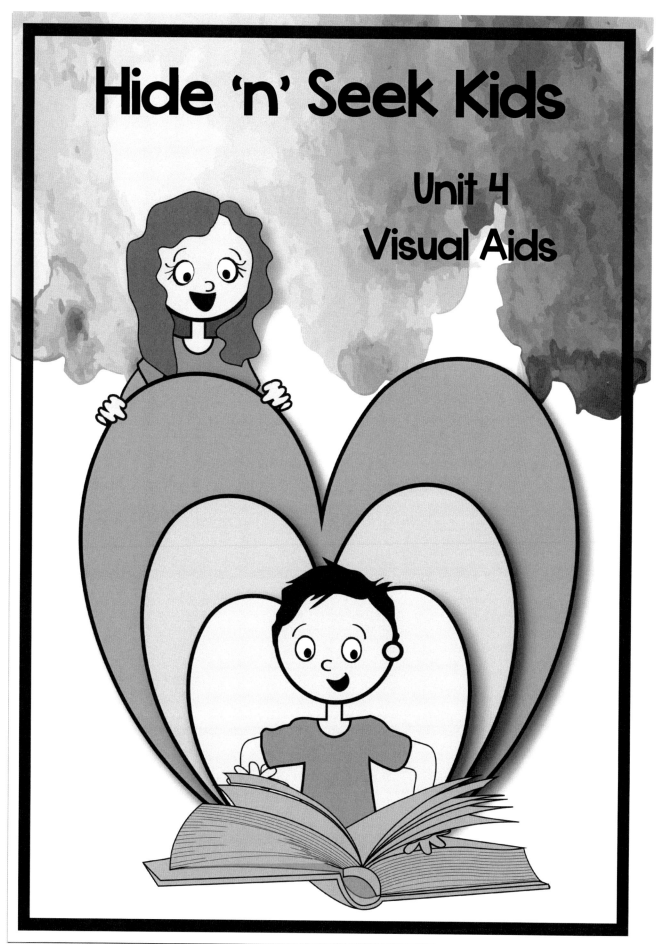

About the Hide 'n' Seek Kids Visual Aids

How Are They Used?

The Hide 'n' Seek Visual Aids book is a companion resource to be used alongside the Hide 'n' Seek Kids Core Curriculum book for each unit. These colorful pictures are used in presenting the key concepts; telling the Bible stories; and, in playing the Bible Story Review games.

What Do They Include?

There are five, different resources included in this book:

1. Key Concept Visual Aids-- colorful signs of the Big Question and Answer, the Bible verse, and the Listening Assignments to use with the 5 lessons for each unit.

2. The Storyboard Picture Key-a who's who of the pictures in thumbnail size. Some pictures are labelled "BG." These are your background pictures that you put on the storyboard before telling the story. The rest of the pictures are labelled "SB." These are pictures you put up on the storyboard as you tell the story.

3. Storyboard Suggested Picture Placement page--where to place the pictures on your storyboard.

4. The pictures, themselves. Notice that each picture is identified and numbered on the back for easy reference. The numbers corrrespond to the numbers in the Picture Placement Key and in the actually story script (found in the Core Curriculum book.)

5. Directions for making the Hide 'n' Seek Kids "Bible" Folder and the **back/front images** to paste in place when making it. (Larger back/front images are found online with the curriculum.)

(Directions for how to make a homemade flannelgraph storyboard and sturdy storyboard pictures are found in **Appendix E in the Core Curriculum book.**)

Ready, Set, Rip It Out!

This book is meant to be ripped up and made into your visual aids. The key concept signs can be cut out and laminated or slipped into sheet protectors. Cut out around the storyboard images and ideally, laminate these. Some of the biggest pictures actually need to be stuck together, before laminating.

Store It!

Hide 'n' Seek Kids is a curriculum that can be used over and over. Store your visual aids and storyboard pictures after using them and they will serve you for many years. We store ours in manilla envelopes and then put them (along with all the rest of the curriculum) in magazine files, labelled by unit. If you have multiple classes using the curriculum, store each set of resources in separate manilla envelopes. This will make prep much simpler, second time around.

Replacement Storyboard Pictures

You can always purchase this book again or simply go online and print out any pictures that go missing.

Two Sizes of Storyboard Pictures

There are two sizes of storyboard pictures to choose from: the standard, large format pictures; or, the smaller format pictures. The larger pictures are best for a big classroom and a storyboard that is at least 36" x 48." (We actually make a whole section of a wall into a felt storyboard!) The small format pictures are created to fit smaller storyboards--in the 24" x 36" to 36" by 48" range. They are most useful in the smaller class or for use at home.

The Case of the Big Showdown
Exodus 1-12

Story-telling Tips

Ahead of time:
1. Read the Bible verses and story. Pray!
2. Choose story action cues and/or prepare storyboard pictures, if using. (Included in Visual Aids book)
3. Practice telling story with the pictures, timing your presentation. Shorten, if necessary to fit your allotted time.

During your presentation:
1. Maintain as much eye contact as possible as you tell the story.
2. Put up storyboard figures/add story action cues as you tell the story. Allow the children to help you put them on the board, if desired.
3. Include the children in your story with a few questions about what they think will happen or words/concepts that might be new to them.
4. Watch the kids for signs that their attention span has been reached. Shorten, if necessary.

INTRODUCTION/ LISTENING ASSIGNMENTS

"Our story is called: The Case of the Big Showdown. Here is your listening assignment... "

Read from Detective Dan's Listening Assignment signs, but questions are summarized below:

Detective Dan's Lesson #1 Listening Assignment:

As you listen to the story, see if you can figure out:
1. A showdown is like a fight to see who's the best. Who won the showdown in this story?
2. What did He prove when He won?

Detective Dan's Lesson #2 Listening Assignment:

Our Bible verse is 1 Kings 8:23: "O LORD... there is no God like you in heaven above or on earth beneath."

As you listen to the story, see if you can figure out:
1. Who didn't believe the LORD was the one, true God in our story?
2. How did the LORD show that He really was the one, true God?

Detective Dan's Lesson #3 Listening Assignment:

I found four clues, but one of them is NOT in the story.
They are: A rug; A frog; A king (Pharaoh); and Moses.
Hold up each of the four pictures for the children to see as you identify them. Better yet, put them up on your flannelgraph board, off to one side.

I need to know:
1. Which three pictures belong in the story and which one does not?
2. How did the LORD use three things to show He was the one, true God?

Detective Dan's Lesson #4 Listening Assignment:

As you listen to the story, see if you can figure out:
1. Who did the LORD prove He was in our story?
2. What was something God's people asked the LORD for and He answered their prayers?

Detective Dan's Lesson #5 Listening Assignment:

As you listen to the story, see if you can figure out:
1. Who did the LORD save His people from in our story?
2. What would He send Jesus to save His people from one day?

Read the questions, THEN SAY,

"Ok, Hide 'n' Seekers! Put on your best listening ears and see if you can find the answers to Detective Dan's questions. When I finish telling the story, we'll see what we come up with."

"The Case of the Big Showdown"   Exodus 1-12

Story with lines separating paragraphs (text in bold, optional interaction cues in italics) Numbers correspond to storyboard pictures and placement upon the storyboard. Alway feel free to use less pictures, if it's best for your kids. Simply, black out the numbers next to pictures you do not plan to use. All pictures are found in the Visual Aids book. Put BG (background) pictures on storyboard ahead of time. SB pictures (listed below in story text) are added to board as you tell the story. These numbers are also found on the back of each picture.
Tip: Stack pictures in numerical order before telling story for easy use. Use sticky-back velcro to attach pictures to storyboard felt. Use sticky-tac putty to stick a picture on top of another picture.

(SB1) God's people were very sad.

What do you look like when you are sad? Can you show me?

A mighty, mean king (SB2) was hurting them. He made them work too hard. He didn't take care of them. He wouldn't let them go home.

"(SB3) Help us, LORD! Help us! DO SOMETHING!" God's people cried out.

Can you help God's people cry out? Say, "Help, us, LORD! Help us! DO SOMETHING!"

The LORD heard the people. He saw what the mighty, mean king did. He knew how sad His people were and He DID something! He sent (SB4) Moses and Aaron to rescue them.

"What do you think the LORD did?"

The LORD told Moses and Aaron to talk to the king (SB5). "The LORD says: 'Let My people go!' they told the king.

Can you tell the mean king the LORD's message? Say: "Let My people go!"

But the mighty, mean king did NOT think the LORD was any god at all. He said, (SB6) "No!" to Moses. "I will not let them go! Instead, I will make the people sadder. I will make them work harder." And he did just that.

Now God's people were even sadder! They worked even harder and hurt even more! There was only one thing to do: "Help us, LORD!" Moses and the people cried out to God. "Help us! DOOOOOO SOMETHING!"

The people were really, REALLY sad now. Let's cry out to God even louder with them: "Help us, LORD! Help us! DOOOOO SOMETHING!"

The LORD heard the people. He saw what the mighty, mean king did. He knew how sad His people were... and He did something AGAIN!

"What do you think the LORD did now?"

The LORD sent sad things upon the mighty, mean king, his people and his land...but protected His people from them all. This would show EVERYONE that He was the One, True God. This would make the king free God's people.

Story with lines separating paragraphs (text in bold, optional interaction cues in italics)

So the LORD sent nasty flies and gnats (SB7) that swarmed and buzzed all around the king and his people...but not a one bothered God's people!

Can you buzz like a fly?

He sent lots of (SB8, SB9, SB10) slippery-slidey frogs to hop all around the king and his people...and even into their houses...even into their beds! But not a one bothered God's people!

Can you hop like a grasshopper?

He sent (SB11) hungry locusts to munch up all the food of the king and his people. He made (SB12) itchy, scratchy, ouchy bumps pop out all over their skin. He made other sad things happen to the king and his people (and (SB13) even to their animals and (SB14) plants. But not a one bothered God's people (SB15) or their (SB16)animals or their plants!

The mean king and his people were very sad and miserable. They didn't like all the things the LORD had sent upon them.

What do you think they looked like?

What would the mighty, mean king do now? Would he believe that the LORD is the One, True God? Now would he let God's people go free? YES, HE WOULD!

"(SB17) Go away! Go home! THE LORD IS GOD!" the mighty, mean king said. "We have had enough of these sad things. We will do what your God wants us to do," he said. "God's people can go free!"

What did the mean king say? "Go away! Go home! The LORD IS GOD!"

How HAPPY (SB18) Moses and Aaron were! How happy God's people were! They (SB19) praised the LORD, the one, true God. He loved them and had heard their cries. He had seen what the mighty, mean king did. He knew how sad His people were... AND HE DID SOMETHING!

God's people were so happy! The LORD rescued them from the mighty, mean king. Let's cheer for God! He's not like anyone else!

How great is the LORD! He is not like anyone else!

Cracking the Case: (story wrap-up for Listening Assignments)

It's time to see how we did with our Listening Assignment.

Detective Dan's Lesson #1 Listening Assignment:
1. A showdown is like a fight to see who's the best. Who won the showdown in this story? The LORD.
2. What did He prove when He won? The LORD showed that He was the one, true God.

For You and Me:
The LORD showed He was the one, true God long ago and He is still the one, true God today. There's no one better to love and obey than Him. His good plans for His people and this world will always win! Let's ask Him to help us to put our trust in Him.

Detective Dan's Lesson #2 Listening Assignment:
Our Bible Verse is 1 Kings 8:23: "O LORD... there is no God like you in heaven above or on earth beneath."

1. Who didn't believe the LORD was the one, true God in our story? The mean, mighty king (Pharaoh) and his people.
2. How did the LORD show that He really was the one, true God? He rescued His people from the mean, mighty king and did it in such great ways that even the king had to say that the LORD is God in heaven and on earth!

For You and Me:
The LORD is still the one, true God. There are none other like Him in heaven or on earth. And the amazing thing is, this great God wants us to be His people! Let's ask Him to help us to turn away from our sins and put our trust in His Son, Jesus as our Savior. He loves to answer this prayer.

Detective Dan's Lesson #3 Listening Assignment:
I found four clues, but one of them is NOT in the story. They are: A rug; A frog; A king (Pharaoh); and Moses.

1. Which three pictures belong in the story and which one does not? The rug was not in the story.
2. How did the LORD use three things to show He was the one, true God? Moses spoke God's words to the king, but the king refused to let the people go or admit that the LORD was God. The LORD used His mighty power and sent lots of frogs and many other things the king did not like. At last, he admitted that the LORD really was the one, true God.

For You and Me:
The LORD is still the one, true God. He wants us all to love Him, know Him and obey Him. We can ask Him and He will help us. What a wonderful thing it is to be one of God's people!

Detective Dan's Lesson #4 Listening Assignment:
1. Who did the LORD prove He was in our story? The one, true God.
2. What was something God's people asked the LORD for and He answered their prayers? They asked God to rescue them.

For You and Me:
God is still the one, true God who wants us to know, love and obey Him. He still loves to rescue His people when they cry out to Him We can be His people when we turn from our sins and trust in Jesus as our Savior.

Detective Dan's Lesson #5 Listening Assignment:
1. Who did the LORD save His people from in our story? The mighty, mean king.
2. What would He send Jesus to save His people from one day? Save them from their sins.

For You and Me:
We might not need to be rescued from a mighty, mean king like God's people did long ago, but we do all need to be rescued from our sins. The LORD wants to rescue us. He sent His Son, Jesus to be our Savior. Jesus can save us from our sins and make us God's people, too, when we repent of our sins and trust in Him as our Savior.

The Gospel (story wrap-up if NOT using Listening Assignments)

Our Bible Truth is:
Can Anybody Tell Me What the LORD Is Like?
He's Not Like Anyone Else!

The LORD is the one, true God. We should all obey Him! But, like the mighty, mean king in our story, we all say "no" to God... and we deserve God's punishment! How sad!

But, oh, how kind is the LORD! If we say sorry to Him and ask Jesus to be our Savior, God will forgive us and save us!

What a wonderful beginning that will be! For then we will get to know God in our hearts. And one day, we will go to live happily with Him forever.

Let's thank God and praise God right now for sending Jesus to save us! Let's ask Him to help us to say sorry to Him and trust in Jesus as our own Savior.

Close in prayer.

Closing Unit 4 ACTS Prayer

A=Adoration C=Confession T=Thanksgiving S=Supplication

A We praise you, God. You are the one, true God in heaven above and here on earth.

C God, in our hearts we know that You are God and that we should obey You, but many times we don't want to. Please forgive us. We need a Savior!

T Thank You for not just being good and great, but being so good and so great to people like us! Thank You for caring about us so much and for wanting us to know You. And thank You so much for sending Jesus to be our Savior.

S Work deep inside our hearts. Help us to turn away from our sins and trust in Jesus as our Savior. Help us to know You and live for You. Help us to go and tell others what we've learned about You, the one, true God.

In Jesus' name we pray. Amen.

Can Anybody Tell Me What the LORD Is Like?

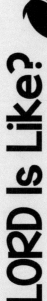

ANSWER:

He's Not Like Anyone Else!

The Big Question

Hold up the Big Question sign for all the children to see, and say:

The Big Question we are investigating today is Big Question Number 4:

Can Anybody Tell Me What the LORD Is Like?

and the Answer is:

He's Not Like Anyone Else!

Meaning:

There are many gods that people worship, but none is like the LORD. He is the one, true God. He's not like anyone else! He's always been alive--and He will never die. He's completely good and loving. He's all-powerful and all-wise. And that's just the beginning of what the LORD is like. He is so great! There will always be more of Him to know.

Let's sing our Big Question Song:"

Big Q & A 4 Song

HSK ESV Songs 4, track 12
(adapted version of "Have You Ever Seen a Lassie")

Can anybody tell me,
Tell me, tell me,
Can anybody tell me,
What the LORD is like?
He's not like anyone else,
Anyone else, anyone else,
He's not like anyone else,
That's what the LORD is like.

"O LORD...there is no God like you....

in heaven above....

VISUAL AID #2

Place verse in HSK Bible Folder — *HSK Bible Folder*

take out of BQB

or on earth beneath." 1 Kings 8:23

HSK 4 Bible Verse Picture--front

Unit 4 Bible Verse

"Who would like to get our Bible verse out of the Big Question Briefcase for me?"

Choose a child to open the briefcase, take out the "Bible" with the Bible Verse in it and hand it to you. Remove the Bible Verse Picture from the "Bible" (held in place by velcro) and hold it up for all the children to see, then say:

1 King 8:23, ESV

"O LORD...there is no God like you, in heaven above or on earth beneath."

Meaning:
The LORD is the one, true God. There is no one like Him, in heaven or earth. Let's praise Him!

"We've said our Bible verse, now let's sing it!"

O, O LORD : I Kings 8:23

HSK ESV Songs 4, track 15

O, O, LORD,
There is no, no God like You,
O, O, LORD,
There is no God like You.
O, O, LORD,
There is no, no God like You,
First Kings Eight, twenty-three.

"Now it's time to do a bit more deep down investigating. Let's read Detective Dan wants us to help him figure out. Would someone like to get it out for me?"

VISUAL
AID
#3

Place verse in **HSK Bible Folder** take out **? Big Question Briefcase ?** of BQB

HSK Bible Folder

Detective Dan's Listening Assignment #1

Detective Dan's Listening Assignment #1

Hi, Hide 'n' Seek Kids!

I'm working on a brand-new case called:

"The Case of the Big Showdown."

I need to find out:

1. A showdown is like a fight to see who's the best. Who won the showdown in this story?

AND

2. What did He prove when He won?

Can you help me? Listen carefully to the story and you might just hear the answers!

Thanks!
Detective Dan

Then say, "Ok, Hide 'n' Seekers! Put on your best listening ears and see if you can find the answers to Detective Dan's questions. When I finish telling the story, we will see if we can answer all of his questions."

Read the Bible Truth story, putting up the storyboard pictures as you tell it. At the end of the story, repeat the questions and lead the children in answering them. Present the gospel and close in prayer.

Answers to assignment questions, the gospel and ACTS prayer are also included at the end of the story text.

Answers:
It's time to see how we did with our Listening Assignment.

Detective Dan's Lesson #1 Listening Assignment:

1. A showdown is like a fight to see who's the best. Who won the showdown in this story? The LORD.

2. What did He prove when He won? The LORD showed that He was the one, true God.

For You and Me:
The LORD showed He was the one, true God long ago and He is still the one, true God today. There's no one better to love and obey than Him. His good plans for His people and this world will always win! Let's ask Him to help us to put our trust in Him.

Place verse in HSK Bible Folder

take out of BQB

HSK Bible Folder

#2

Detective Dan's Listening Assignment #2

Detective Dan's
Listening Assignment #2

#2

Hi, Hide 'n' Seek Kids!
I'm still working on the case called:
"The Case of the Big Showdown."

Our Bible verse is I Kings 8:23:
"O LORD... there is no God like you in heaven above or on earth beneath."

I need to find out:
1. Who didn't believe the LORD was the one, true God in our story?
AND
2. How did the LORD show that He really was the one, true God?

Can you help me? Listen carefully to the story and you might just hear the answers!

Thanks for your help!
Detective Dan

Then say, "Ok, Hide 'n' Seekers! Put on your best listening ears and see if you can find the answers to Detective Dan's questions. When I finish telling the story, we will see if we can answer all of his questions."

Read the Bible Truth story, putting up the storyboard pictures as you tell it. At the end of the story, repeat the questions and lead the children in answering them. Present the gospel and close in prayer.

Answers to assignment questions, the gospel and ACTS prayer are also included at the end of the story text.

Answers:
Our Bible Verse is 1 Kings 8:23: "O LORD... there is no God like you in heaven above or on earth beineath."

1. Who didn't believe the LORD was the one, true God in our story? The mean, mighty king (Pharaoh) and his people.

2. How did the LORD show that He really was the one, true God? He rescued His people from the mean, mighty king and did it in such great ways that even the king had to say that the LORD is God in heaven and on earth!

For You and Me:
The LORD is still the one, true God. There are none other like Him in heaven or on earth. And the amazing thing is, this great God wants us to be His people! Let's ask Him to help us to turn away from our sins and put our trust in His Son, Jesus as our Savior. He loves to answer this prayer.

Detective Dan's
Listening
Assignment #3

Detective Dan's Listening Assignment #3

Hi, Hide 'n' Seek Kids!

I'm still working on the case called:

"The Case of the Big Showdown."

I found four clues, but one of them is NOT in the story. They are: A rug; A frog; A king (Pharaoh); and Moses.

Hold up each of the four pictures for the children to see as you identify them. Better yet, put them up on your flannelgraph board, off to one side.

I need to know:

1. Which THREE pictures belong in the story and which ONE does NOT?

AND

2. How did the LORD use three things to show He was the one, true God?

Can you help me? Listen carefully to the story and you might just hear the answers!

Thanks!
Detective Dan

Then say, *"Ok, Hide'n'Seekers! Put on your best listening ears and see if you can find the answers to Detective Dan's questions. When I finish telling the story, we will see if we can answer all of his questions."*

Read the Bible Truth story, putting up the storyboard pictures as you tell it. At the end of the story, repeat the questions and lead the children in answering them. Present the gospel and close in prayer.

Answers to assignment questions, the gospel and ACTS prayer are also included at the end of the story text.

Answers:

1. Which three pictures belong in the story and which one does not? The rug was not in the story.

2. How did the LORD use three things to show He was the one, true God? Moses spoke God's words to the king, but the king refused to let the people go or admit that the LORD was God. The LORD used His mighty power and sent lots of frogs and many other things the king did not like. At last, he admitted that the LORD really was the one, true God.

For You and Me:
The LORD is still the one, true God. He wants us all to love Him, know Him and obey Him. We can ask Him and He will help us. What a wonderful thing it is to be one of God's people!.

Rug

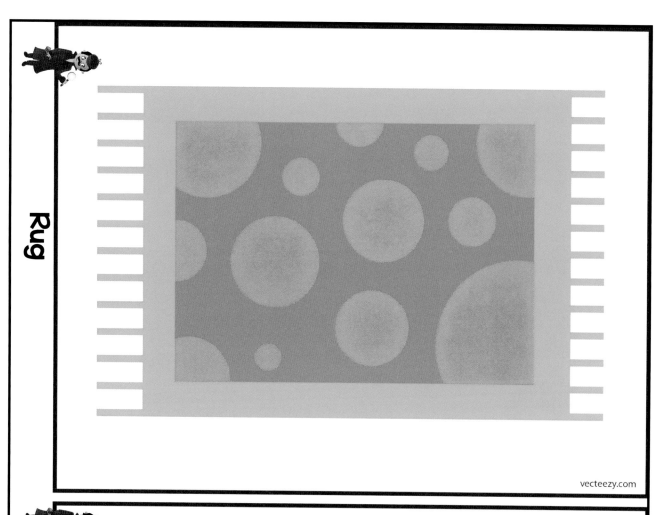

vecteezy.com

Frog

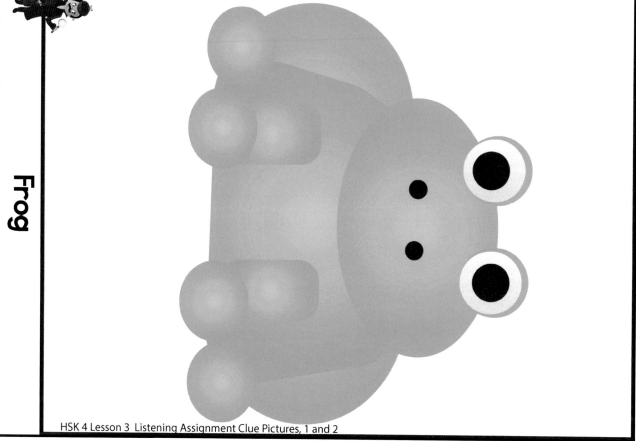

VISUAL AID #5B

Place verse in   take out

HSK Bible Folder

HSK Bible Folder   of BQB

HSK 4 Lesson 3 Listening Assignment Clue Picture1 for kids

VISUAL AID #5B

Place verse in   take out

HSK Bible Folder

HSK Bible Folder   of BQB

HSK 4 Lesson 3 Listening Assignment Clue Picture 2 for kids

218

King (Pharaoh)

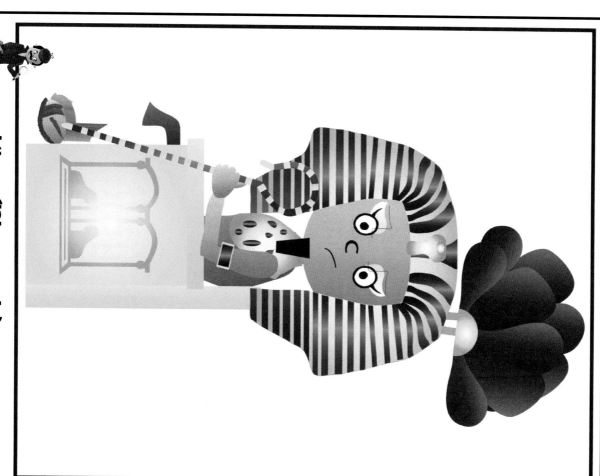

Moses

VISUAL
AID

#5C

*Place
verse in*   *take out*

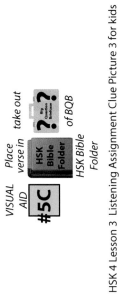

HSK
Bible
Folder   *of BQB*

*HSK Bible
Folder*

HSK 4 Lesson 3 Listening Assignment Clue Picture 3 for kids

VISUAL
AID

#5C

*Place
verse in*   *take out*

HSK
Bible
Folder   *of BQB*

*HSK Bible
Folder*

HSK 4 Lesson 3 Listening Assignment Clue Picture 4 for kids

VISUAL
AID
Place
verse in
take out
of BQB

#6

HSK Bible
Folder

#4

Detective Dan's
Listening
Assignment #4

Detective Dan's
Listening Assignment #4

Hi, Hide 'n' Seek Kids!

I'm still working on the case called:
"The Case of the Big Showdown."

I need to find out:
1. Who did the LORD prove He was in our story?
AND
2. What was something God's people asked the LORD for and He answered their prayers?

Can you help me? Listen carefully to the story and you might just hear the answers!

Thanks!
Detective Dan

Then say, "Ok, Hide 'n' Seekers! Put on your best listening ears and see if you can find the answers to Detective Dan's questions. When I finish telling the story, we will see if we can answer all of his questions."

Read the Bible Truth story, putting up the storyboard pictures as you tell it. At the end of the story, repeat the questions and lead the children in answering them. Present the gospel and close in prayer.

Answers to assignment questions, the gospel and ACTS prayer are also included at the end of the story text.*

Answers:
1. Who did the LORD prove He was in our story? The one, true God.
2. What was something God's people asked the LORD for and He answered their prayers? They asked God to rescue them.

For You and Me:
God is still the one, true God who wants us to know, love and obey Him. He still loves to rescue His people when they cry out to Him We can be His people when we turn from our sins and trust in Jesus as our Savior.

Detective Dan's Listening Assignment #5

#5

Detective Dan's
Listening Assignment #5

#5

Hi, Hide 'n' Seek Kids!

I'm still working on the case called:
"The Case of the Big Showdown."

I need to find out:

1. Who did the LORD save His people from in our story?
AND
2. What would He send Jesus to save His people from one day?

Can you help me? Listen carefully to the story and you might just hear the answers!

Thanks!
Detective Dan

Then say, "Ok, Hide 'n' Seekers! Put on your best listening ears and see if you can find the answers to Detective Dan's questions. When I finish telling the story, we will see if we can answer all of his questions."

Read the Bible Truth story, putting up the storyboard pictures as you tell it. At the end of the story, repeat the questions and lead the children in answering them. Present the gospel and close in prayer.

Answers to assignment questions, the gospel and ACTS prayer are also included at the end of the story text.*

Answers:
1. Who did the LORD save His people from in our story? The mighty, mean king.
2. What would He send Jesus to save His people from one day? Save them from their sins.

For You and Me:
We might not need to be rescued from a mighty, mean king like God's people did long ago, but we do all need to be rescued from our sins. The LORD wants to rescue us. He sent His Son, Jesus to be our Savior. Jesus can save us from our sins and make us God's people, too, when we repent of our sins and trust in Him as our Savior.

HSK 4 Storyboard Picture Key: Background Pictures (BG)

Put these pictures in place on your storyboard BEFORE you tell your story.

BG1 Egyptian Background

BG2 King's Palace

Store these pictures in numerical order in your HSK Bible Folder.
Add these to your story as you tell it. Numbers correspond to placement order.

SB1 God's people Sad, Working Hard and Getting Hurt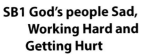

SB12 Egyptian People with Boils

SB2 Mighty, Mean King (Pharaoh)

SB13 Egyptians' Sick Animals

SB3 God's People Praying

SB14 Egyptians Dying Plants

SB4 Moses and Aaron

SB15 God's People Happy, with No Sickness

SB5 Mighty, Mean King Talking to Moses and Aaron

SB16 God's People's Animals and Plants with No Sickness

SB6 "No"

SB17 "Go Away"

SB7 Flies and Gnats

SB18 "The LORD Is King, the One, True God"

SB8 Frogs

SB19 Moses and Aaron Rejoicing

SB9 and SB10 Frogs on Everything

SB11 Locusts

Note: Use sticky tac putty rather than velcro on back of pictures placed on top of other pictures.

HSK 4 Bible Story: The Case of the Big Showdown

Suggested Picture Placement

NOTE:
Some of the larger images are assembled from two or more pages. You can make these easier to fold by leaving a small gap in the lamination between the pieces. This allows you to fold the image along the gap.

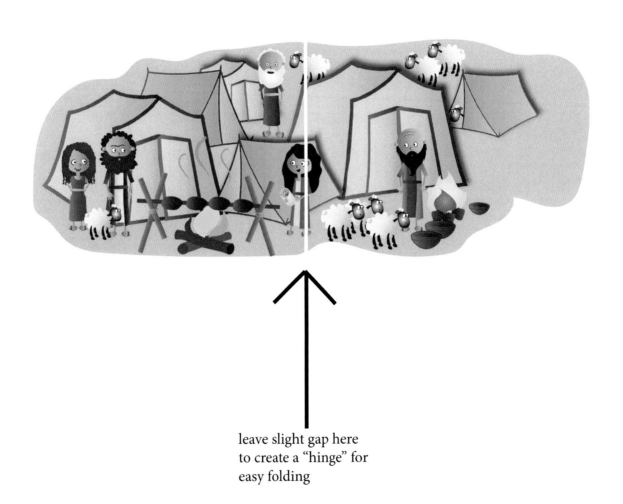

leave slight gap here
to create a "hinge" for
easy folding

**BG 1 Egyptian Background,
pg 1 of 2** HSK 4 Story
glue together, then laminate
Put on board ahead of time

BG 1 Egyptian Background, pg 2 of 2 HSK 4 Story
glue together, then laminate
Put on board ahead of time

BG2 Palace, pg 1 of 2
HSK 4 Story
glue together, then laminate
Put on board ahead of time

235

BG2 Palace, pg 2 of 2
HSK 4 Story
glue together, then laminate
Put on board ahead of time

SB1 God's people working hard, sad and getting hurt, pg 1 of 2
HSK 4 Story
glue together, then laminate

**SB1 God's people working hard,
sad and getting hurt, pg 2 of 2**
HSK 4 Story
glue together, then laminate

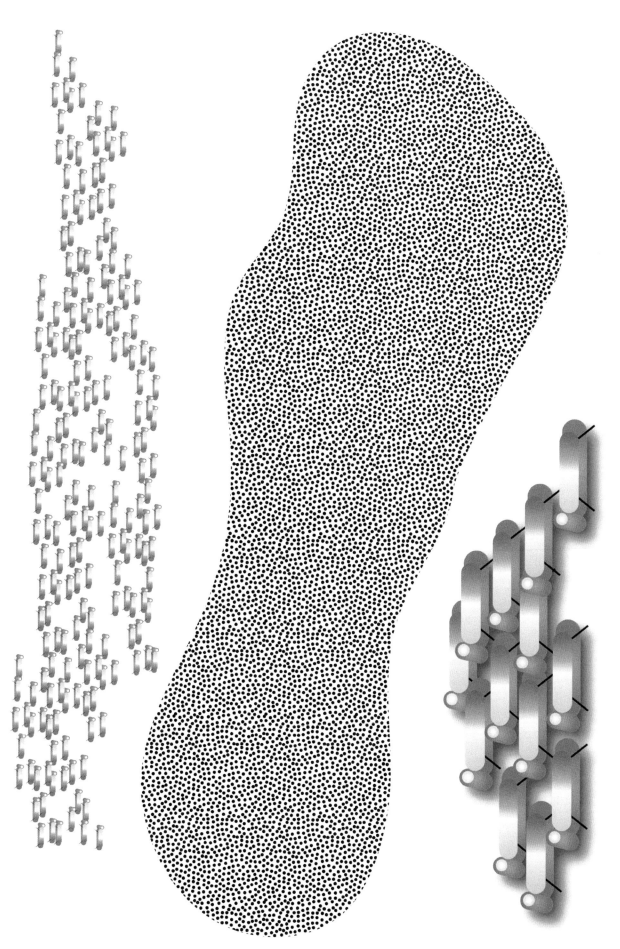

SB7 Gnats and Flies
HSK 4 Story

SB11 Locusts
HSK 4 Story

SB13 Egyptians' Sick Animals

HSK 4 Story

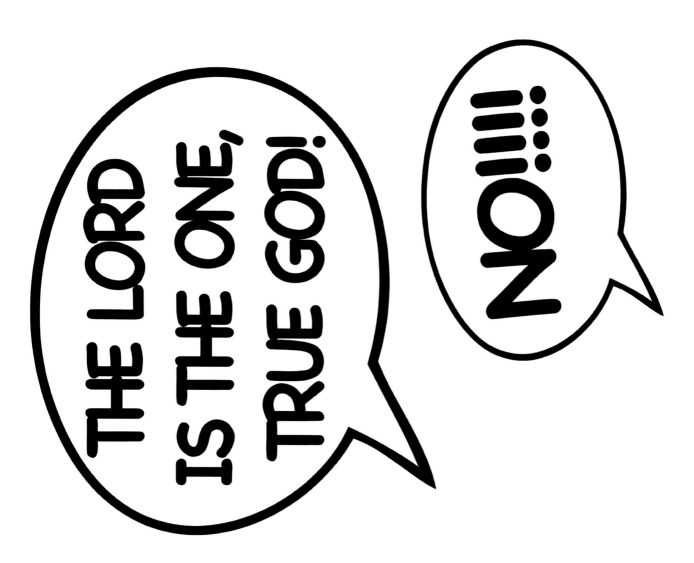

SB18
The LORD Is the One, True God
HSK 4 Story

SB6 "No"
HSK 4 Story

SB17 "Go Away"
HSK 4 Story

SB3
God's People Praying to God
HSK 4 Story

SB15
God's People Happy, with No
Sickness

HSK 4 Story

251

SB19 Moses and Aaron Rejoicing
HSK 4 Story

SB5 Mighty, Mean King (Pharaoh) talking to Moses and Aaron
HSK 4 Story

SB4 Moses and Aaron
HSK 4 Story

SB8 Frogs
HSK 4 Story

SB16 Healthy Animals and Plants of God's People

HSK 4 Story

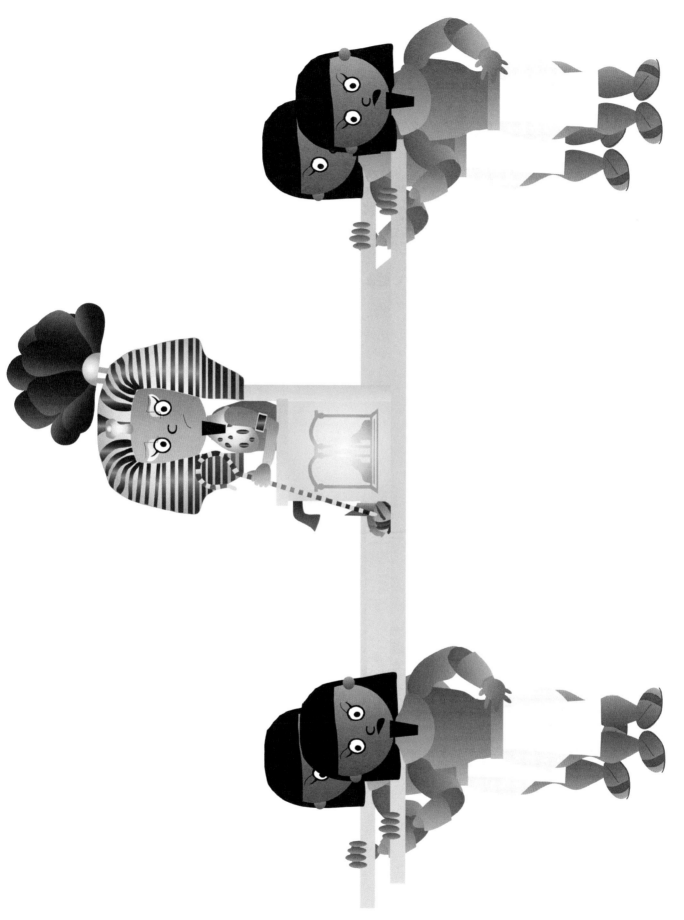

SB2
The Mighty, Mean King (Pharaoh)
HSK 4 Story

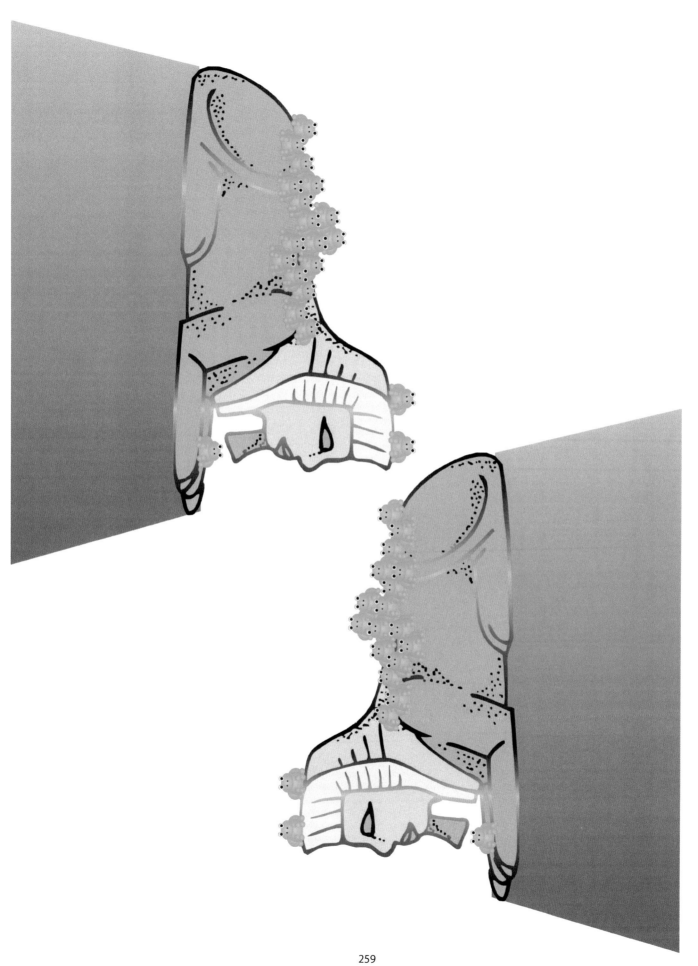

SB9 Frogs on Everything 1
HSK 4 Story

SB10 Frogs on Everything 2
HSK 4 Story

SB12 Egyptian People
with Boils

Hide 'n' Seek Kids

Other Visual Aids

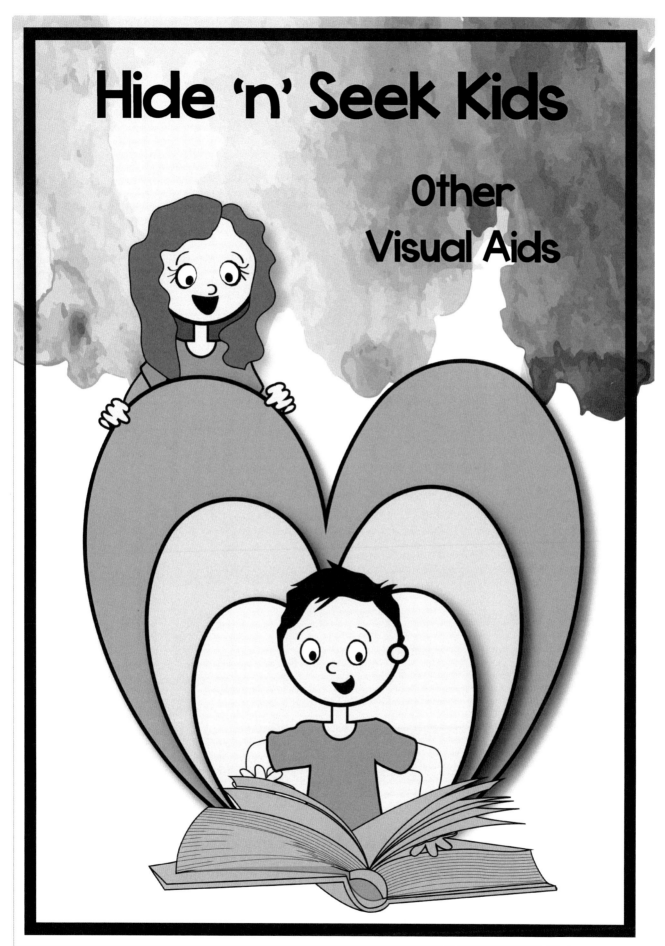

The Hide 'n' Seek Kids "Bible" Folder

This is a homemade folder that looks (kinda) like the cover of a Bible. You will use this to put the Bible verse, the Bible Story and storyboard pictures to help make the point that the truths you are teaching them come from the Bible.

Supplies
1 piece of 22" x 28" posterboard (white is fine. Green or brown is nice)
Glue
Stapler and staples or packing tape
The Bible Cover pictures (see online with resources for this unit or from the back of each Hide 'n' Seek Kids Visual Aids book.)

NOTE: The Bible Cover pictures included in the Hide 'n' Seek Kids Visual Aids books cannot be created larger than 8.5" x 11". That means that they will be under-sized for a Bible Folder of the dimensions you are making. However, you can go online to the Hide "n' Seek Kids curriculum and there is a pdf of a bigger version of these covers that will actually fit the size of this HSK "Bible" Folder.

Directions
1. Lay out poster board with long side along the bottom.

2. Fold in 2" on each side.

3. Take packing tape and tape the folded in 2" flaps to the main section of the posterboard, all the way down.

3. Fold up 8 1/2" on the bottom of the poster board.

4. Use packing tape to tape this flap in place, all the way down.

5. Take scissors and snip through the tape where the flap is attached to the folder. This will give you a bit more room in the folder.

6. Fold the poster board in the middle to make the center fold.

7. Cut out the Bible Cover Pictures. If possible, laminate these. They will last longer.

8.. Glue the two cover pieces to the outside of the folder.

28" side

22" side

2"

2"

8 1/2"

Holy
Bible

HSK "Bible" Outside Front

HSK "Bible" Outside Back

Making a Flannelgraph Storyboard
for use in story-telling and in playing the story review games

While you may decide to use sticky tac and stick your storyboard pictures to a white board, it is very easy to make a flannelgraph board. The advantage to the flannelgraph board is that the pictures stick very easily and there is no messing with the sticky-tac.

Supplies
Large Format Pictures Board: AT LEAST a 36" x 48" foamboard or corkboard (We actually use a far bigger canvas and attach it to the wall) A science project board with the two sides that fold out makes a good 36" x 48" board.
Small Format Pictures Board: AT LEAST a 24" x 36" (to 36" x 48)" board
Large piece of neutral-colored felt to cover your board with extra to overlap over to the back, if desired.
Glue gun and glue sticks

Directions
1. Center felt on front side of board. Turn over. Secure in place with glue.

Making Durable Storyboard Pictures
for use in story-telling and in playing the story review games

Whether you purchase the Hide 'n' Seek Kids storyboard pictures from Amazon or print them off the website (included in the Hide 'n' Seek Kids Visual Aids book), you will want to find some way to make them more durable. They are used not only as a part of telling the story, but are integral in the story review games. Here's how we make ours durable enough to be used over and over again.

Supplies
Hide 'n' Seek Kids Visual Aids book (purchased or downloaded)
White cardstock or printer paper (if downloading pictures)
Sticky-back velcro, circles or cut pieces; or sticky tac putty
Laminator or Self-laminating sheets
Sturdy Sheet Protectors, preferably the "Secure Top" kind, like offered by Avery
Flannelgraph pictures for the Bible stories found at www.praisefactory.org with each unit's resources.

Directions
1. Purchase from Amazon or download and print out the storyboard figures.

2. Cut out flannelgraph figures.

3. Laminate the figures.

Special tip: When laminating the big background pictures that are two (and sometimes even three or four) pieces put together, leave a small gap between the two pieces before laminating together. This small space acts like a hinge and allows you to fold up pictures without hurting them into a manilla envelope that fits 8.5" x 11" sheets of paper along with all of the smaller, regular-sized storyboard pictures.

4. If using a flannelgraph board: Stick a piece of sticky backed velcro (ROUGH SIDE) onto the back of each figure. If using sticky tack and whiteboard: simply stick a small amount of sticky tack on the back of a picture when using it. Remove and store sticky tack in airtight container.

Big Question Box/Briefcase

What You Want

The Big Question Briefcase is a briefcase or other container with these characteristics:

- Ideally, this should be around 17" x 12", but needs to be at least big enough to fit a 8 ½" x 11" sheets of paper inside it.
- Have various pockets to put these sheets in
- Is attractive or curious looking to preschoolers
- Not necessary, but extremely fun, if is has a combination lock

Finding a Briefcase:

You can certainly buy one new, but you always may find a used one at a thrift shop. Or, someone may have one they want to donate. We use one that stores valuables in it and is the 17" x12" size. Very durable and has the lock feature that the kids love.

You also can move away from the briefcase idea and use a little trunk or other box for your substitute briefcase. Just change the name to the Big Question Box, if you use a box instead. A boot box or the cardboard box that 10 reams of copy paper comes in is a great size, if you are using a box.

If you use a box, but want a lock-like feature, that's easy to do. Simply cut "straps" out of felt or vinyl and glue in place to the top and bottom sides of the box on one side, with the top strap overlapping the bottom straps. Add velcro to the top and bottom pieces so that they meet and fasten. Make back "hinges" for the box with the felt/vinyl straps, too. Or, you can simply add a belt around the box that has to be unfastened before the box can be opened.

Here are some suggestions for decorating a box or even the outside of your briefcase to make it appealing.

Supplies

Your box/briefcase
Plain white contact paper or white cardstock
Colorful wrapping paper
Glitter glue
Markers
Sequins, fake jewels, buttons, rick rack, etc.
Other decorating supplies
Stickers
Glue
Clear packing tape

Directions

1. If you are using a box that has wording on it, you will first need to make plain surfaces for decorating and a hinge for the lid. Stick the white contact paper or white cardstock to each side of the box. On the other hand, you can also use colorful wrapping paper. Then, make a lid by sticking the clear packing tape along one long side of the box, attaching the lid to the box.

2. Use the craft decorating supplies to decorate the box. If desired, you can put a big question mark on top of the box, but remember that you are working with two and three year olds: the question mark symbol is not very meaningful to them yet.

Made in the USA
Middletown, DE
18 June 2019